THE GOURMET FOOD STORAGE HANDBOOK

STEPHANIE PETERSEN

FRONT TABLE BOOKS | SPRINGVILLE, UTAH

ISBN 13: 978-1-4621-1199-2

Published by Front Table Books, an imprint of Cedar Fort, Inc.
2373 W. 700 S., Springville, UT 84663
Distributed by Cedar Fort, Inc., www.cedarfort.com

LIBRARY OF CONGRESS CATALOGING-IN-PUBLICATION DATA

Petersen, Stephanie.
The gourmet food storage handbook / Stephanie Petersen.
pages cm
ISBN 978-1-4621-1199-2
1. Cooking, American. 2. Cooking--Utah. 3. Brand name products--Utah--Brigham City.
I. Title.
TX715.P4785 2012
641.59792--dc23
2012035125

Cover and page design by Erica Dixon

Edited by Casey J. Winters

Printed in China

10 9 8 7 6 5 4 3 2 1

To my husband and children, who love me unconditionally and have been very sweet about taste testing all these amazing recipes.

To my master gardening–genius father and food science–genius mother, who raised me with my feet in dirt and my hands in bread dough.

Finally, to my grandma Barbara who taught me to dehydrate food and cook with grains. She was the original gourmet food storage expert, long before it was popular.

CONTENTS

BEANS

Bean Recipes

52 METHOD: MEALS IN A JAR

Recipes for the 52 Method: Dinner Meals

WHOLE GRAIN BREADS

DESSERTS

Candy Making

GOURMET MIXES

Variations on All-Purpose Baking Mix

Variations on Honeyville Pancake Mix

HOLIDAY SOUP MIXES

GLUTEN-FREE

FOREWORD

WHAT YOU ARE HOLDING IN YOUR HANDS is the culmination of several years of practical, hands-on cooking advice that I have used as a chef, mom, and friend. It is the basic field guide of recipes that I have used in teaching thousands of men and women how to be more self-reliant and save a lot of money cooking with grain and food storage. It is an outstanding everyday resource to have when you just want to make the basics or when you want to make something elegant. I use these recipes on a daily basis to feed my own family, so I know that they not only work but also taste wonderful.

WRITING THIS BOOK

When Honeyville first approached me about writing their company food storage cookbook, it was, for me, the ultimate compliment. I've loved Honeyville grains and flours since I was a child. When I grew up and became a pastry chef, I adored their flours even more! I have come to know them as a company that provides the highest quality grain products and food storage supplies to people all over the world. It is an honor to be their chef and work with them in developing recipes. Make no mistake about it; Honeyville is the finest you can buy. I've been able to use the entire Honeyville product line while writing this book, including premium grains, grain blends, specialty flours, seeds, freeze-dried products, dehydrated foods, drink mixes, and powdered dairy items. These things should be on hand for quick, money-saving meals. If you've never cooked with food storage, this book is for you. If you're experienced using food storage, this book will expand your recipe base and give you a more gourmet edge. You may not realize what you actually have in your pantry! I'm here to help you see the magnificent gift that food storage can and should be. Prepare to be dazzled!

MY PERSONAL EXPERIENCE

Many years ago I set aside my work in the gourmet kitchen to take on the full-time task of being a mother. When my son was born, I knew I needed to be home with him. We lived on a tight budget, and I made everything from scratch that I possibly could so that ends would meet and I could be there for the big events. When my baby took his first steps and fell, he said, "Mama." I knew I was on the right track.

Looking back now, I see that those were golden years, tender moments, and experiences that I will never forget. Those were also years of being in the "refiner's fire" when it came to cooking and baking. I found myself milling my own flour from whole grain, working on an organic tomato farm to get extra groceries, learning how to make yogurts and cheeses from powdered milk, and cooking with a solar oven. Anything that would save money and still make food remarkable, I found a way to do it! It wasn't always easy, but I know now that it was a priceless experience. You cannot teach what you do not know or haven't experienced yourself. I know how to cook on a budget. I know how to use food storage every single day. I've lived it!

THE NEED TO SHARE

Many years into my food-storage experience, a dear friend and bishop at church asked me if I would be willing to teach a few gals how to cook. It seems that there was a great need for others to learn what I already knew about food storage. I accepted the challenge and invited girls over to my home during the week to cook with me. I found an unbelievable satisfaction in helping to build the experience of these dear friends, and soon that desire to share led to starting a food blog. That need to share has never ended. You are holding in your hands the first of many cookbooks that I hope to write on this subject. When you open it, you are opening my heart. Enjoy. I say it every time I teach a class in Honeyville stores or film a new tutorial segment: "Welcome to the Honeyville kitchen."

APPETIZERS

STEAMED CORN CUSTARD WITH BUTTERED CRAB OR SHRIMP

For custard

- 1 cup Honeyville freeze-dried sweet corn
- 1/3 cup Honeyville whole milk powder
- ½ cup water
- 2 Tbsp. Honeyville powdered whole eggs
- ¼ tsp. salt

For crab topping

- ½ cup king crab meat or ½ cup shrimp (fresh preferred, but canned will work)
- 1 Tbsp. Honeyville powdered butter
- 1 Tbsp. chopped fresh chives

Special equipment: 4 (2-oz.) ceramic or glass ramekins

Directions: To make custard, pulse corn in a spice blender or mill until a powder. Add milk powder, ½ cup water, powdered eggs, and salt. Whisk well and divide among 4 ramekins. Steam custards in a steamer set 1 inch above simmering water, covered with lid, until centers are set and a thin knife inserted into center of custard comes out clean, 6–8 minutes. Remove ramekins from steamer with tongs and cool custards slightly.

Make crab topping while custard cools: Coarsely chop crab meat or shrimp meat. Heat the meat in a lightly oiled skillet. Add the powdered butter and cook about 2 minutes. Stir in chives. Serve custards topped with crab or shrimp. I'm not going to lie. It is amazing!

YIELDS 4 SERVINGS.

The sweetness of the corn coupled with the lightly salty taste of fresh shrimp or crab is almost too deliriously delicious! Serve this warm as a nibble before a meal. You'll find it to be a light, refreshing touch.

MINI CHEESE AND ONION QUICHE

¾ cup crushed saltine crackers

¼ cup melted butter

nonstick cooking spray

¾ cup Honeyville dehydrated green onions

2 Tbsp. Honeyville powdered butter

Honeyville Ova Easy whole egg crystals (equal to 2 eggs plus water)

1 cup prepared Honeyville powdered sour cream

½ tsp. salt

¼ tsp. pepper

1 cup Honeyville freeze-dried cheddar cheese

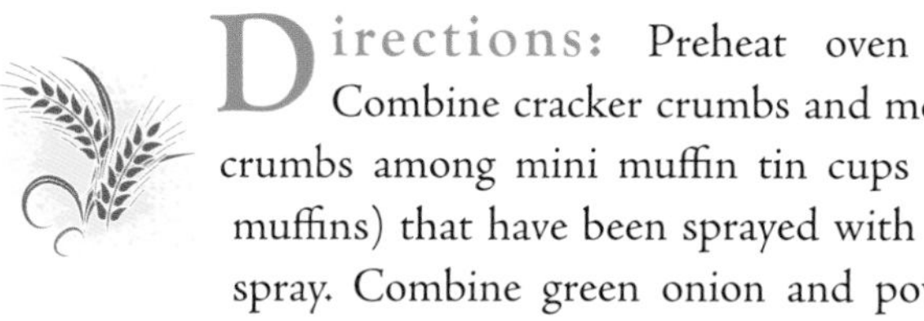

Directions: Preheat oven to 300 degrees. Combine cracker crumbs and melted butter. Divide crumbs among mini muffin tin cups (24 one-inch mini muffins) that have been sprayed with a nonstick cooking spray. Combine green onion and powdered butter and divide evenly on top of cracker crumbs. Beat eggs, sour cream, salt, pepper, and cheese. Pour by spoonfuls on top of onions in tins. Do not fill to top, as they will run over. Bake until set, 15–20 minutes. Do not overbake.

YIELDS 24 MINI QUICHE.

This is the classic addition to any appetizers table or menu. There must be mini-quiche. This is a fun recipe that you make in mini muffin cups. I sometimes skip the bottom crust altogether and just put a mini Ritz cracker on the bottom of the pan. It works perfectly!

ITALIAN WHITE BEAN DIP WITH TOASTED PITA CHIPS

2 cups cooked cannellini beans, drained and rinsed

2 cloves garlic

2 Tbsp. fresh lemon juice

⅓ cup olive oil, plus 4 Tbsp.

¼ cup (loosely packed) fresh Italian parsley leaves

¼ cup (loosely packed) basil leaves

salt

freshly ground black pepper

6 pitas

1 tsp. Chef Tess Romantic Italian seasoning

Directions: Preheat oven to 400 degrees. Place the beans, garlic, lemon juice, ⅓ cup olive oil, parsley, and basil in the work bowl of a food processor. Pulse until the mixture is coarsely chopped. Season with salt and pepper. Transfer the bean puree to a small bowl. Cut each pita in half and then into 8 wedges. Arrange the pita wedges on a large baking sheet. Pour the remaining oil over the wedges. Toss and spread out the wedges evenly. Sprinkle with Romantic Italian seasoning. Bake for 8–12 minutes or until toasted and golden in color. Serve the pita chips warm or at room temperature alongside the bean puree.

YIELDS 2 CUPS DIP.

This is an exceptionally delicious, elegant, and budget-friendly appetizer to serve at any party. I love this white bean dip as an Italian sandwich spread as well!

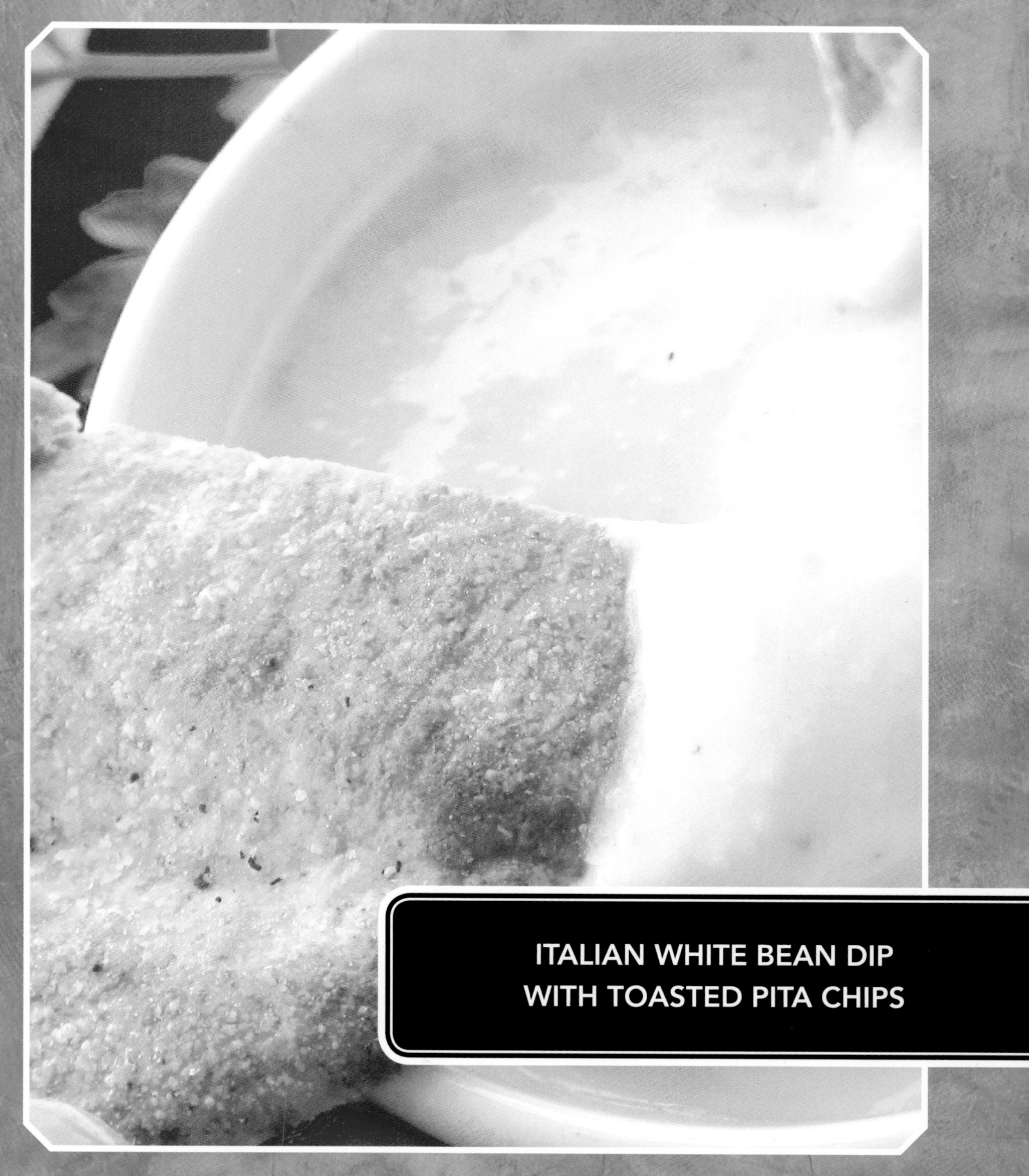

ITALIAN WHITE BEAN DIP WITH TOASTED PITA CHIPS

ORANGE GINGER BBQ CHICKEN WRAPS

2 Tbsp. light-colored oil, such as vegetable oil or peanut oil

3 cups Honeyville freeze-dried chicken, hydrated and drained well

2 cups Honeyville freeze-dried mushrooms, hydrated and drained well

coarse real salt

coarse black pepper

3 cloves garlic, chopped, or 2 tsp. dry garlic

1 inch ginger root, finely chopped or grated, optional

1 orange, zested (for dry zest, use 1 Tbsp. and pulverize to a powder)

½ cup Honeyville freeze-dried bell peppers

1 small (6–8 oz.) tin sliced water chestnuts, drained and chopped

3 Tbsp. Honeyville dehydrated green onions

½ cup hoisin sauce (Chinese barbecue sauce available in Asian foods aisle of most grocery stores)

½ large head iceberg lettuce or romaine lettuce, core removed, head quartered (for romaine, just leave whole)

wedges of navel orange

for garnish

Directions: Preheat a large skillet or wok to high. Add oil to hot pan. Add chicken to the pan. Add mushrooms and cook another minute or two. Add salt and pepper to season, then garlic and ginger. Cook a minute more. Grate zest into pan; add bell pepper bits, chopped water chestnuts, and green onions. Cook another minute, continuing to stir fry mixture. Add hoisin Chinese barbecue sauce and toss to coat the mixture evenly. Transfer the hot chopped barbecued chicken to serving platter and pile the quartered wedges of crisp iceberg lettuce along side. Add wedged oranges

to platter to garnish. To eat, pile spoonfuls into lettuce leaves, wrapping lettuce around fillings, and squeeze an orange wedge over it.

YIELDS 6 SERVINGS.

SWEET CORN AND AVOCADO SALSA (COWBOY CAVIAR)

1 ripe avocado, cut into ¼-inch dice

3 Tbsp. fresh lime juice

1 (15–oz.) can diced fire-roasted tomatoes, drained

1½ cups Honeyville freeze-dried corn, hydrated

1 cup cooked Honeyville black beans or white beans, well drained

¼ cup Honeyville dehydrated green onion or 1 fresh green onion, chopped)

1 jalapeño pepper, seeded and minced (for a hotter salsa, leave the seeds in)

¼ cup chopped fresh cilantro (2 Tbsp. dehydrated)

coarse salt (kosher or sea)

freshly ground black pepper

2 tsp. Chef Tess Southwest Fajita seasoning

Directions: Place the avocado in the bottom of a non-reactive mixing bowl and gently toss it with lime juice. Add remaining ingredients, stirring gently. Taste for seasoning, adding more lime juice as necessary, and season with salt and pepper to taste. The salsa should be highly seasoned. This can be made up to 24 hours in advance if you add the avocado just before serving (so it doesn't brown).

YIELDS 2–3 CUPS.

FRENCH ONION DILL DIP MIX

- ½ cup Honeyville dehydrated onion
- ½ cup Honeyville dehydrated green onion
- ½ cup Honeyville powdered sour cream
- ½ cup Honeyville powdered butter
- 1 Tbsp. granulated garlic
- 2 Tbsp. dill
- 1 Tbsp. black pepper

Directions: Place the onion in a dry skillet. Cook over medium heat 4–5 minutes until brown but not burned. Allow to cool. Combine all ingredients.

YIELDS 3 CUPS MIX.

TO MAKE THE DIP: Combine 3 Tbsp. onion dill dip mix, 1 cup sour cream, and ¾ cup mayonnaise (may use fat-free varieties). Chill at least 3 hours. May add bacon, Honeyville freeze-dried cheddar cheese, and so on.

SUN-DRIED TOMATO DIP

¼ cup sun-dried tomatoes in oil, drained and chopped (8 tomatoes)

1 (8–oz.) pkg. cream cheese, at room temperature

½ cup yogurt (unsweetened)

½ cup mayonnaise

10 dashes of hot red pepper sauce

1 tsp. kosher salt

¾ tsp. freshly ground black pepper

2 scallions, thinly sliced (white and green parts)

2 tsp. Chef Tess Romantic Italian seasoning

Directions: Puree the tomatoes, cream cheese, sour cream, mayonnaise, red pepper sauce, salt and pepper in a food processor fitted with a metal blade. Add the scallions and pulse twice. Serve at room temperature.

PINEAPPLE CHEESE BALL

2 (8-oz.) pkgs. cream cheese

½ cup milk or cream

1 cup Honeyville freeze dried cheddar cheese

¼ cup Honeyville freeze dried celery (not dehydrated)

½ cup Honeyville freeze dried onion (or ⅓ cup dehydrated onion)

½ cup Honeyville freeze dried pineapples, hydrated according to directions, chopped, drained

2 tsp. Chef Tess All Purpose Mix seasoning

Directions: Allow cream cheese to soften to room temperature. In a large bowl, combine all ingredients, whipping well, about 2 minutes. Scrape cheese mixture out of bowl and form into 2 rough balls. Put on a plate and cover with plastic or a glass cake cover. Chill in the fridge 2–4 hours before serving. I think it's best after 24 hours.

YIELDS 2 AVERAGE-SIZED CHEESE BALLS.

CROSTINI WITH GOAT CHEESE AND GARLIC-APPLE CHUTNEY

CROSTINI WITH GOAT CHEESE AND GARLIC-APPLE CHUTNEY

For chutney:

- 1 cup brown sugar
- ¾ cup apple-flavored balsamic vinegar or regular apple cider vinegar
- 4 cloves pressed garlic
- 2 tsp. fresh minced ginger
- pinch of cayenne
- 3 cup Honeyville freeze-dried apple (plus 1 cup water)
- 1 cup golden raisins or dried cranberries
- 1 cup plum tomatoes, peeled, diced, and seeded

For crostini:

- 1 baguette, cut into ⅓-inch-thick slices
- olive oil
- 12 oz. soft fresh goat cheese or homemade yogurt cheese

Directions: Combine all chutney ingredients in a non-reactive half-gallon pot with a heavy bottom and simmer 10–15 minutes until apples are hydrated and mixture is thick like a jam.

TO MAKE CROSTINI: Preheat oven to 450 degrees. Arrange baguette slices on baking sheet and brush with olive oil. Bake until golden and crisp, about 8 minutes. Spread each piece of toast with goat cheese. Top with chutney.

I'm not going to lie; my husband, Ace, ate an entire batch of this appetizer on his own! I always know when I have a winner! This one is a great balance of savory and sweet with a light salty tang from the goat cheese. You will find it to be a fast favorite in your family.

Breakfasts

ODE TO KATE SWEET CREPES FROM FOOD STORAGE

½ cup Honeyville powdered whole eggs

1 cup Honeyville all-purpose flour

1 Tbsp. sugar

⅓ cup Honeyville instant powdered milk

½ tsp. salt

¼ tsp. Chef Tess Wise Woman of the East spice blend

2 cups water

2 tsp. vanilla

Directions: Combine dry ingredients in a large bowl. Add water and vanilla. Blend in blender or really well by hand with a whisk. Lightly oil an 8-inch nonstick pan and put over medium-low heat. If your pan is too hot, the crepe batter will start to cook before you can coat the pan with it. Scoop ¼ cup batter into pan and just roll the pan around until the batter lightly coats the bottom of the pan. Cook 2–3 minutes on one side and then gently turn over. Cook the crepe a minute or two more. Slide the crepe out of the pan and repeat until all the crepe batter is used. Fill crepes with fresh fruit, cottage cheese, or cream cheese and drizzle with a sweet sauce.

YIELDS 12 CREPES.

Iy friend Kate sent ne her food storage ecipe for crepes. I've dapted the recipe bit, but I have to ive her credit for the nitial recipe and the lea of using food torage to make these emarkable crepes. 'hank you, Kate!

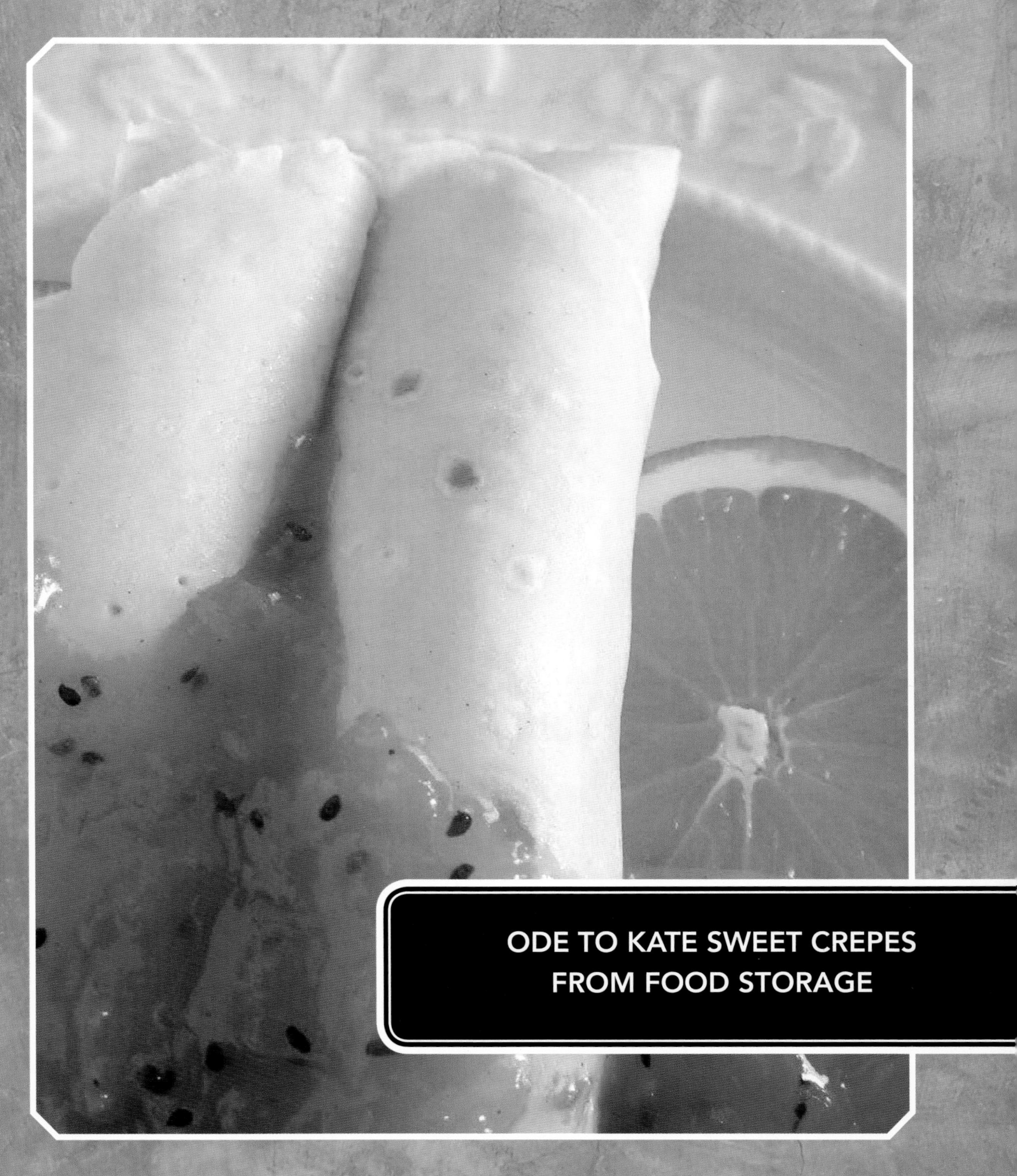

ODE TO KATE SWEET CREPES FROM FOOD STORAGE

BISCUIT QUICHE MUFFINS

Crust:

- 1 cup Honeyville all-purpose flour
- 1¼ tsp. baking powder
- ½ tsp. salt
- 2 Tbsp. shortening or butter
- ¼ cup plus 2 Tbsp. cold water or milk

To prepare crust: In a medium bowl, combine the flour, baking powder, and salt. With a fork, cut the shortening or butter into the flour, blending until the pieces of fat are very small. Add the cold water or milk to the flour mixture. Mix lightly and then lightly sprinkle flour onto a countertop to keep the dough from sticking. With a rolling pin, roll out the dough to ½-inch thickness. Cut 12 two-inch circles with a biscuit cutter. Lightly oil a muffin tin and place the dough in the bottom of each cup, like a crust.

Breakfast should be fun! Kids love these little grab-n-go, snack-size breakfast cups. They're a cross between a biscuit and a quiche!

Filling:

- 4 scoops Honeyville Ova Easy egg crystals equal to three eggs, hydrated
- 1 Tbsp. Honeyville powdered butter (dry)
- 1 Tbsp. Honeyville powdered sour cream (dry)
- ½ cup Honeyville freeze-dried ham, hydrated with ½ cup hot water
- ¼ cup Honeyville freeze-dried bell pepper, chopped fine
- ½ tsp. Chef Tess Romantic Italian seasoning
- 2 cups Honeyville freeze-dried Colby cheese, hydrated

Directions: Preheat oven to 425 degrees. Combine eggs, dehydrated butter, and dehydrated sour cream until well combined. Put pieces of ham and bell pepper in each cup. Fill cup with 1 tablespoon filling mixture. Sprinkle with Romantic Italian seasoning. Put a little cheese on top of biscuit quiche muffins. Bake for 13–15 minutes. Serve warm.

Yields 12 muffins.

BANANA-NUT BREAD 4-GRAIN CEREAL

HOMEMADE INSTANT CEREAL PACKETS

ONE PLAIN PACKET:

- ⅓ cup Honeyville 4-grain cereal mix
- 1 Tbsp. Honeyville oat bran or ground flax seed

Directions: Combine ingredients. To serve, add ½ cup boiling water and allow to sit for 3-4 minutes. Use more or less water depending on how thick or thin you like your cereal.

FLAVOR-ADD-IN VARIATIONS FOR EACH PLAIN PACKET

BANANA-NUT BREAD 4-GRAIN CEREAL PACKET

To Plain Packet above, add

- 3 Tbsp. Honeyville dehydrated honey
- 1 tsp. Mix-a-Meal butterscotch powder
- 3 Tbsp. Honeyville freeze-dried bananas
- 1 Tbsp. toasted chopped walnuts (optional)

Directions: Add ⅔ cup boiling water to contents and let sit 3–4 minutes.

Sugar and spice and everything...amazing! You won't find these flavors in the premade packets from the store. I have some hearty eaters in my family who want whole-grain breakfast with the added benefits of fiber! This is a surefire way to add some nutrition and also have a quick grab-n-go breakfast! I put each of my cereal mixes in snack-size zip-sealing baggies. Two baggies will fit in a pint jar for longer-term storage. One serving stored in a half-pint jar is perfect for when I want to have breakfast in a convenient container ready to add boiling water. Cost effective, nutritious, and outstandingly tasty!

SPICED PEACHES AND CREAM COBBLER 4-GRAIN CEREAL PACKET

To Plain Packet (pg. 21), add

- 3 Tbsp. Honeyville freeze-dried peaches
- 2 Tbsp. Honeyville Peaches and Cream Smoothie Mix
- ¼ tsp. Chef Tess Wise Woman of the East spice blend

Directions: Add ⅔ cup boiling water and let it sit for 3–4 minutes.

MAPLE-CRANBERRY PECAN 4-GRAIN CEREAL PACKET

To Plain Packet (pg. 21), add

- 2 Tbsp. Honeyville granulated honey
- ¼ tsp. Mix-a-Meal powdered maple flavor
- 3 Tbsp. chopped toasted pecans
- 2 Tbsp. Honeyville dried cranberries

Directions: Add ½ cup boiling water and allow to sit 3–4 minutes.

SPICED VANILLA–ORANGE ROLL 4-GRAIN CEREAL PACKET

To Plain Packet (pg. 21), add

¼ tsp. Chef Tess Wise Woman of the East spice blend

2 Tbsp. Honeyville vanilla pudding powder

1 Tbsp. Honeyville granulated honey

½ tsp. dry orange zest (or ¼ tsp. Mix-a-Meal powdered orange flavor)

Directions: Add ½ cup boiling water and allow to sit 3–4 minutes.

BERRIES AND BAVARIAN LEMON CREAM 4-GRAIN CEREAL PACKET

To Plain Packet (pg. 21), add

3 Tbsp. freeze-dried berries of your choice (I crush them up a bit before I measure them)

2 Tbsp. Honeyville wild berry smoothie mix

1 tsp. Honeyville lemonade powder

Directions: Add ⅔ cup boiling water and allow to sit for 3–4 minutes.

TROPICAL WHITE CHOCOLATE MACADAMIA NUT 4-GRAIN CEREAL PACKET

To Plain Packet (pg. 21), add

- 2 Tbsp. Honeyville Tropical Monsoon smoothie mix
- 1 Tbsp. white chocolate chips
- 1 Tbsp. chopped Macadamia nuts

Directions: Add ½ cup boiling water to contents and let sit 3–4 minutes.

Beans

BEANS 101

Let's talk about the magical food: beans. I teach basic cooking skills as well as advanced culinary arts. That's what I do. I'm a firm believer that you may never know when you will be called upon to cook a staple food or a fancy dish. Knowing the basics of something as simple as beans is something you will never regret. You may know how to make painted breads, but honestly, that isn't a daily need unless you run a bakery. You will always have to feed yourself or your family. Sometimes things may be financially tight, or you may be looking for a lean nutritional main dish. Food-wise, you can't go wrong with beans. Their nutritional data can't be beat, especially fiber and calories when it comes to filling up hungry bellies and staying full! Beans are an amazing food . . . unless, of course, you don't cook them correctly. Then you have crunchy, bean-shaped things in sauce . . . that frankly aren't very appealing. It reminds me too much of eating bugs. Yes, I also ate bugs as a kid. I know that explains a lot. As for beans, what you really want is this tutorial.

BASIC BEANS

1 lb. dry beans (pinto, black, white, black-eyed peas, kidney, and so on)

water

1 Tbsp. baking soda (optional)

Flavor options I use:

pepper

bay leaf

salt-free seasoning

garlic

onion

2 roasted, diced green chilies

Step 1:

Wash and soak* beans. Rinse with hot water and make sure there are no rocks or foreign matter in with your beans. Let's face it, they come from plants . . . there might be dirt. Clean it up. I soak my beans in a gallon of water with 1 tablespoon of baking soda. I have found this step most useful in helping to break down the acids in the bean skins. They cook softer. After 8–24 hours of soaking, I drain the water, rinse the beans again, and put them in a slow cooker or the pot for my solar oven. Either one works, but most people don't cook solar.

*Note: You don't have to soak beans, but it shortens the cooking time and helps with digestion "issues," if you know what I mean. I think you do. You can "quick soak" beans by pouring boiling water over the beans and soaking 1 hour.

Step 2:

Place drained beans in 4-quart slow cooker or 6-quart stovetop pot. Cover beans with 6–8 cups very hot water and simmer. No salt is best at this point. No tomato products either. Salt added at this point will make the beans take longer to cook. Acid products like tomatoes will make it hard to cook, period. To be sure, use just the water and the beans. If you use chicken stock to cook beans, it adds flavor. Just be sure it's low sodium. Okay . . . I say that and then I realize I use black pepper and bay leaf at this point as well. So it's okay to add Spanish seasoning like whole cracked black pepper, bay leaf, ground cumin, dry oregano, ground coriander (about ½ tsp. each), just not the salt until the end. Fair? You can also add a whole onion, with the "paper" skin removed, in with the beans. It sounds strange, but a Mexican gal I love showed me that trick and it's great for adding onion flavor without adding any chunks of onion . . . if you don't want chunks. Just remove the onion after cooking and discard. I've also done this with a whole carrot and a whole celery stalk when I just want to add the flavor. You can also just add the dry onion, garlic, or dry vegetables, again being sure there isn't salt. Yes, I know there are a lot of people who add pig to the beans. Salt pork, bacon, and ham all add salt and a nice smoky flavor. Do what you want. It will take a little longer (by 1–2 hours) if you add a lot of the salted meats. Add 3–4 drops of liquid smoke and you don't have to add meat at all. For black beans, I also add a dash of allspice; believe it or not, I really like the flavor in black beans.

Step 3:

Simmer 1½ hours on stovetop or 2½ hours on high in the slow cooker (3 hours in the solar oven). If you cook them on low temperature, it will take 4–5 hours. If you cook on the stovetop, you may need to add additional water—be sure it is very hot or the cooking time will increase. Yes, you can pressure cook beans—they take 20 minutes that way, but that's another lesson.

⁂ Step 4:

Season. When cooking time is up, check to see if beans are soft before you add the salt and any additional seasoning blends that may have salt in them. This is also where I add roasted, diced green chilies to my beans. Two large, fresh-roasted chilies—peeled, seeded, and chopped—add immense flavor. If you can only find the cans of chilies, use 1–2 small cans of diced green chilies. If you want to add tomato products, you may do so if the beans are tender. Continue to simmer a few minutes. Now this next part may just be me. I love a pronounced flavor of garlic in my beans, so I add it last. I prefer fresh-pressed garlic and use two cloves in my pot. If you want a hint of garlic but not a bold statement, then you can add it at the beginning of cooking.

Homemade beans on a homemade tortilla. This is dinner for pennies. It's not fancy, but it may not be fancy you need. It may be just making it to the next paycheck without feeling deprived of good food. This, my friends, is my gift to you. Enjoy a few more dollars back in your pocket. Fire up the slow cooker or the solar oven and start your pot of beans.

ONE LAST NOTE

Because beans are so high in protein, at the right temperature they are the perfect breeding ground for food-borne illness. Please be sure to cool them quickly. I put my beans in smaller bowls and leave the top vented when I cover them with foil so they will get cold quickly in the fridge. If you freeze them, be sure to cool them in the fridge first and then transfer them to the freezer, so as to not overwork your freezer and keep the beans at a safe temperature. One pound of dry beans will usually yield about 7 cups of cooked beans. That's enough for a family, easily! Serve that with Tess-a-Roni (pg. 94) or regular rice... and you've done it.

BEEFY BBQ BEANS WITH CHEDDAR GARLIC DROP BISCUITS

- 1 onion, chopped
- ½ cup chopped celery
- ½ cup chopped carrots
- 1 Tbsp. oil
- 1 cup Honeyville freeze-dried ground beef, rehydrated
- 1 clove fresh garlic, pressed
- 2 tsp. Chef Tess All Purpose seasoning mix
- ½ cup Honeyville honey barbecue sauce
- 1 large (20-oz.) can organic baked beans or 4 cups homemade baked beans

Biscuit ingredients:

- 1 cup Honeyville flour
- 1¼ tsp. baking powder
- ½ tsp. salt
- 2 Tbsp. shortening or butter
- ½ cup Honeyville freeze-dried cheddar cheese
- 1 tsp. pressed fresh garlic
- ¼ cup plus 2 Tbsp. cold water or milk

Directions: In a 12–inch, covered skillet, sauté onions, celery, and carrots in oil until very dark brown. Add the hamburger and cook until browned. Add the garlic, Chef Tess All Purpose seasoning, Honeyville honey barbecue sauce, and baked beans. Stir well. Lower to a simmer. In a medium bowl, combine the flour, baking powder, and salt. With a fork, cut the shortening or butter into the flour, blending until the pieces of fat are very small. Add the cheese and pressed garlic to the dry ingredients.

Stir in the cold milk or water. Drop by rounded tablespoon on top of the barbecue beef mixture. Cover and simmer on low 12–15 minutes until biscuits are cooked. Top with extra cheese and All Purpose seasoning if desired.

POLYNESIAN-STYLE SWEET AND SOUR WHITE BEANS

- 1 lb. small white navy beans (soaked overnight in 1 gallon water and 1 Tbsp. baking soda, drained, and rinsed)
- ½ cup Honeyville dehydrated onion (or 1 cup fresh)
- ¼ cup Honeyville freeze-dried bell pepper (or ½ cup fresh)
- 4 cups boiling water
- ¼ cup Honeyville jalapeño jelly
- 3 cloves garlic (or 1½ tsp. granulated)
- ⅓ cup hoisin sauce
- ⅓ cup rice vinegar
- 2 tsp. sesame oil or ½ tsp. liquid smoke
- 8 oz. crushed, drained pineapple
- ½ cup chopped fresh cilantro (optional)
- salt and pepper to taste

Directions: Place drained beans in a slow cooker (or solar oven pot) and add onion. Add chopped bell peppers. Add boiling water and simmer on low for 3–4 hours. If you use a solar cooker, it will take the same amount of time in direct sunlight. When beans are tender, add jalapeño jelly. Then add the garlic, hoisin sauce, sesame oil or liquid smoke, pineapple, and fresh cilantro. Cook 5–10 minutes more if desired. I serve it up on a warm bed of jasmine rice with some chopped cilantro and finely chopped red cabbage for garnish if desired.

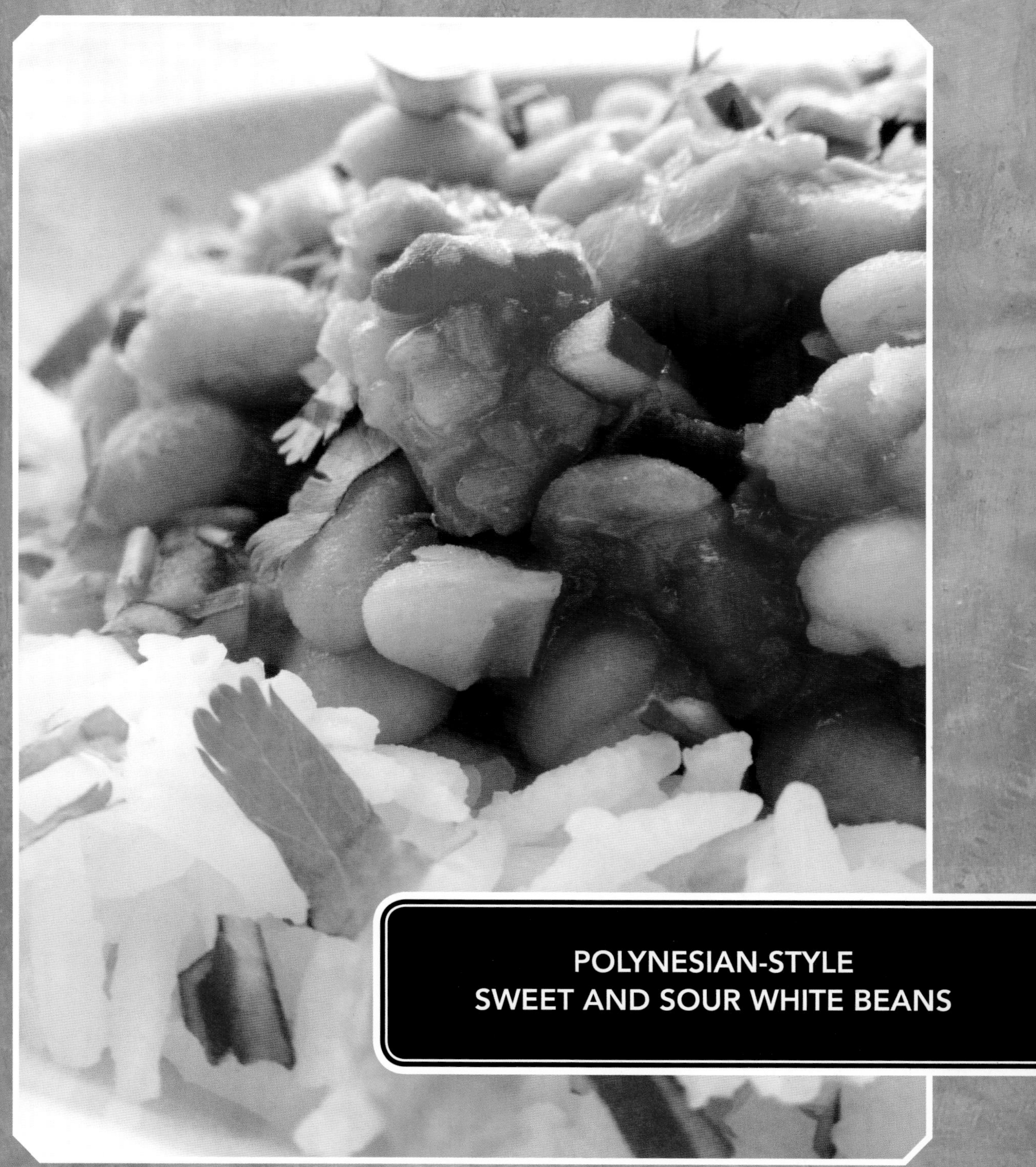

POLYNESIAN-STYLE SWEET AND SOUR WHITE BEANS

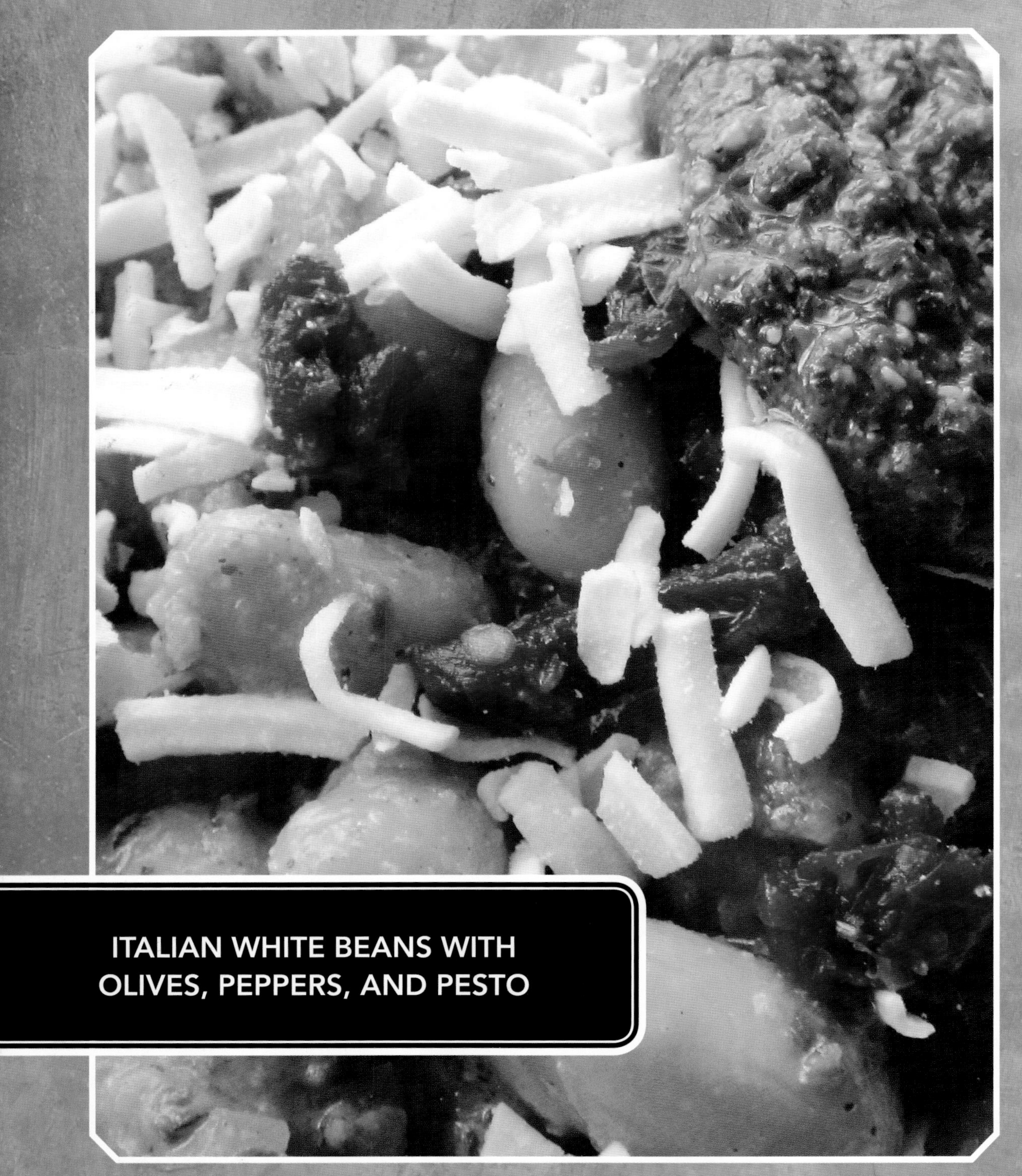

ITALIAN WHITE BEANS WITH OLIVES, PEPPERS, AND PESTO

ITALIAN WHITE BEANS WITH OLIVES, PEPPERS, AND PESTO

1 lb. white beans, cooked until tender (about 6 cups total)

1 cup hot water

½ cup Honeyville dehydrated onion

½ cup Honeyville freeze-dried bell peppers

¼ cup basil pesto, purchased or homemade

2 Tbsp. mixed olive tapenade (chopped olive dip, available by the canned olives)

black pepper and lemon juice to taste

Directions: Combine all ingredients and simmer until veggies are tender, about 10 minutes. Serve hot with crusty Italian bread and fresh-minced rosemary or oregano.

THAI BLACK BEANS IN SPICY PEANUT SAUCE

- 1 lb. Honeyville black beans, soaked overnight (or quick soaked)
- 6 cups water
- ½ cup Honeyville dehydrated onion or 1 cup chopped onion
- 2 Tbsp. minced garlic
- 1 Tbsp. sesame oil
- ⅓ cup vinegar
- ⅓ cup soy sauce
- ¼ cup Honeyville dehydrated peanut butter
- 2 tsp. chile flakes
- 2 tsp. minced ginger
- ½ cup chopped green onions for garnish
- ½ cup chopped fresh cilantro for garnish

Directions: Place beans in a large stockpot with water and simmer until tender (2–3 hours). In a large skillet, sauté onion and garlic in sesame oil. When onion is tender, add vinegar, soy sauce, peanut butter, chile flakes, and ginger. Add sauce to tender beans and simmer 10 minutes. Just before serving, garnish with green onions and cilantro.

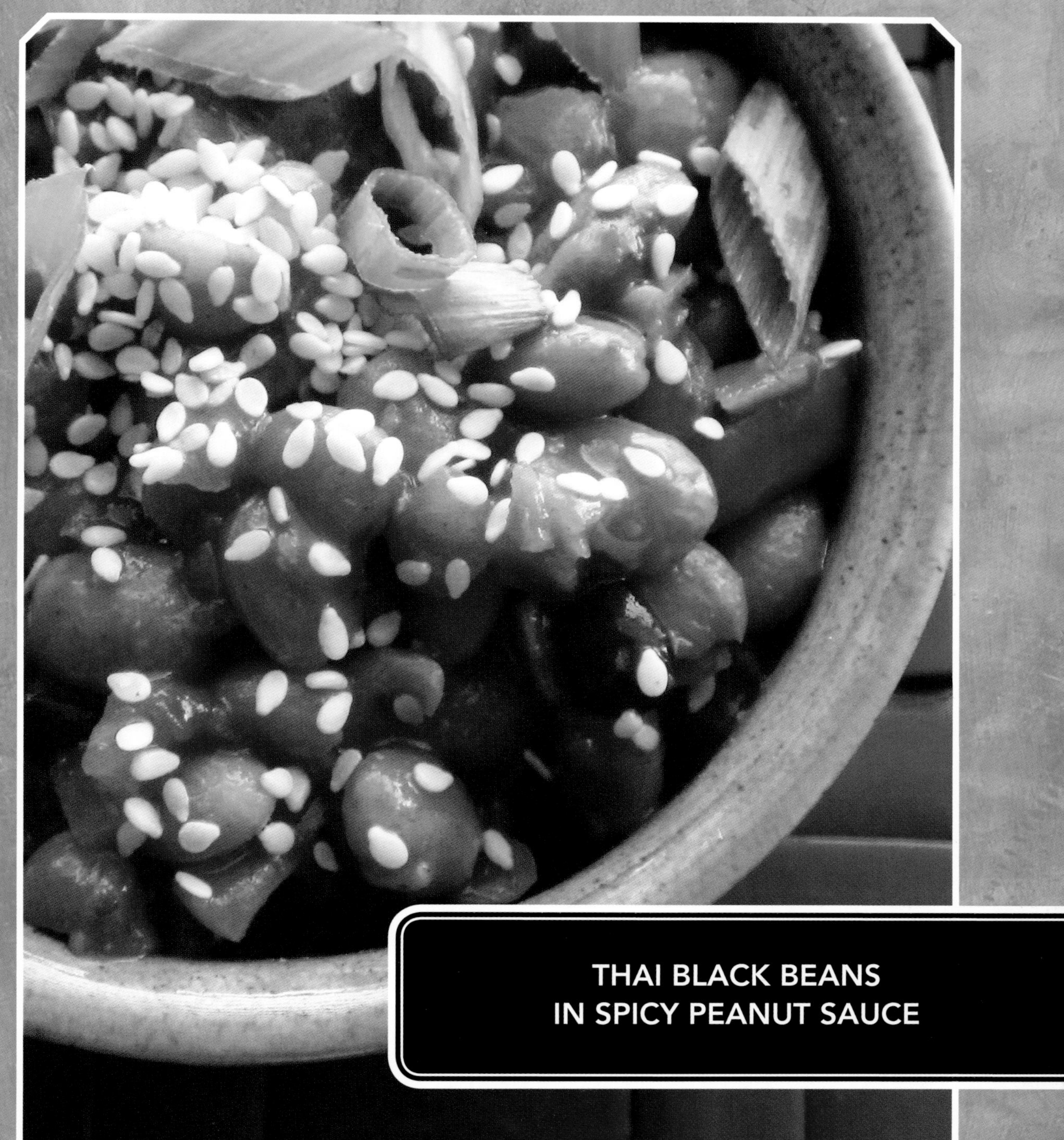

THAI BLACK BEANS IN SPICY PEANUT SAUCE

FRENCH WHITE BEANS AND HAM

- 1 lb. cooked white beans (about 6 cups total) (Mortgage Lifter beans pictured)
- 1 cup hot water
- ¾ cup Honeyville freeze-dried ham
- 1 Tbsp. herbs de Provence (dry French herb seasoning)
- 1 clove fresh garlic, pressed
- ¼ cup sun-dried tomatoes
- ¼ cup Honeyville dehydrated butter
- 3 Tbsp. chopped fresh parsley

Directions: Simmer all ingredients together until ham is hydrated, about 15 minutes. Serve hot with crusty French bread.

52 Method: Meals in a Jar

CONVENIENCE MEAL PLANNING FOR EMERGENCY AND EVERYDAY FOOD STORAGE

This has been one of my most popular classes at the Honeyville Teaching Kitchen because it literally simplifies food storage down to the meals a normal family will actually eat. This is the outline from the classes I teach, along with some new recipes never before shared in the Honeyville Kitchen. I've loved being their company chef and creating this menu plan.

RECIPES AND INSTRUCTIONS

Recently someone asked me to write down a few of my recipes for long-term storage and what I do. I have a method that I like to use that isn't new, but it was a little bit exciting when I heard it. I planned 7 meals, 1 for each night of the week, and then figured out how to get 52 of each meal in my food storage to have on hand. In this way I would easily be able to have a year's supply of food that my family would eat should I need it. Initially I knew I could do it with 52 jars of spaghetti sauce and 52 lbs. of spaghetti noodles. It was a simple way to calculate a family's needs. It's also a good way to get back to the basics of what a normal family will eat. However, I quickly found that living in a tiny condo and trying to remember where I had stored the sauce and the noodles became a problem. Especially several years into the project, getting the food storage and keeping track of cans and locations got tedious. Then I had a stroke of genius. One day I was making soup mix, and I put the entire contents of the mix into a quart-size jar. I wondered why I had not planned my whole food storage this way. As time went on, that simple concept stuck in my mind.

I wanted my menu plan to be concise and in one spot. I didn't want to go searching for the sauce and the noodles or any of the ingredients for a meal on my food storage menu. The shelf life needed to be around 5 to 7 years. The meals had to be simple enough that my kids could make them without my help. That would also spill over into dad being able to make these meals. He knows how to boil water, I'll give him that much. I took on a challenge, but I loved it! Over time, I started developing recipes that would allow me to fit everything for a meal in 1 quart-size jar. I also planned on each one having an "add water only" rule. I didn't want to have to find oil, butter, sugar, a can of tomatoes, or anything else. The first time I shared this concept with an emergency preparedness enthusiast, I got such a remarkable response that I decided maybe, just maybe, this would be something that others would use.

During this time I started to look at home canning safety in depth. Without getting into a lot of canning details and crazy stuff here, I do want to say that I don't want to have to worry about canning meat or rotating cans of beans and vegetables. When I was introduced to freeze-dried fruits and vegetables along with the dehydration methods used for things like sour cream and butter, I cheered! Hooray! I finally had all that I needed to really develop these meals! I've found that buying freeze-dried vegetables and meat has been a much better approach for our family. When food is freeze dried, 97 percent of the nutritional value of the food is preserved. It's a healthy way to approach food.

I'm often asked what I serve with the meals. Generally we plan on a side dish to go with a meal during good times and there is always enough grain figured into my food storage to plan on 2–3 loaves of bread a day. This is in addition to the jars. My family is used to baking bread from whole grain, and we eat pretty modestly. I also try to add fresh garden produce in the form of a salad whenever I can. However, in an extreme emergency, the meal is more than enough for my family. You'll need to try the meals yourself and plan accordingly. I'm sharing with you what has worked for us. We have 2 adults and 2 preteen boys. We also have my husband's parents with us, and they eat pretty light. Is there really enough to serve 4–6 people a real amount of food? Yes. The jars will make between 6 and 9 cups of cooked food, depending on the recipe.

DO YOU HAVE TO USE AN OXYGEN ABSORBER?

Oxygen "eater" packets are used to make meals shelf stable. These will cause a vacuum seal and an oxygen-free environment that will not allow the growth of mold and spores. The jars should be packed in a dry jar on a day when the air has very low humidity. That becomes especially important when repacking freeze-dried meats. Note: It is important to open the freeze-dried meat and bottle it again within 24–48 hours in a very dry environment. If you're worried about it or want a vegetarian alternative, you may use 1½ cups freeze-dried zucchini instead of the meat. You'll need to add 1 tsp. no-MSG chicken bouillon to the mix as well. It is not a good idea to seal these meals in just a plastic storage bag or one that is not designed for long-term storage if you are using the real meat. I'm especially conscious of that. Please don't risk getting your family sick. I can't be held liable for your bad choices.

If you decide to use 12 recipes in your food storage and if you are mixing and matching these jar meals 5 times a week (that leaves 2 days for leftovers or something different) for a year, you will eat each recipe only twice a month (actually 1.66 if you want to be precise). This keeps it fairly fresh and nonrepetitive!

Or just use a few to start off with and see how you like (or love) them! They are so easy to use with the "just add water and boil/bake" directions. Please remember that when you put the oxygen packet on top of the jar, top with a new canning lid, and hand-tighten the band, the button on the lid should depress, confirming that all oxygen has been absorbed and the jar is sealed. You may omit the oxygen packet if you use a jar sealer (such as a FoodSaver). In that case, I put a cupcake liner at the top of the jar just inside the lid to keep the dry ingredients from being sucked into the FoodSaver. The smaller "meal saver" is not made to be used with a jar attachment. Please check with the manufacturer of your vacuum sealer products to be sure they are safe for this form of food storage.

I'm also including some of my breakfast choices. These I use as a breakfast or brunch in long-term emergency preparedness. It's a great way to plan on a breakfast that isn't just plain oatmeal every morning! That being said, here are some of my favorite quart-size-jar recipes that are easily used for long-term emergency food storage or everyday use. All are made in a quart-size jar unless indicated otherwise. Enjoy.

FREQUENTLY ASKED QUESTIONS

HOW DO I GET ALL THE INGREDIENTS TO FIT IN THE JAR?

Many times, I include a lot more ingredients than one would think could fit in a jar. The dry powder ingredients I shake into the vegetables, grain, pasta, or meat. In this way, I'm not only able to reduce the amount of air in a jar, which will help with the shelf life, but I can also make the meal more compact for long-term storage. Shake the jars with the lids on, if necessary. You'll be surprised how much will actually fit.

WHAT SIZE JAR SHOULD I USE?

These recipes can easily be cut in half and used for smaller families. We've done pint-size jars for families with just two adults and had enough for dinner and leftovers to take to work the following day. Single people can make the meals in a half-pint jar, and each recipe will make 4 meals with plenty of food! You will have to adjust the cooking time and amount of water to adjust for these changes. I generally use a wide-mouth quart-size Mason jar.

CAN I USE A MYLAR BAG FOR THESE MEALS?

Yes, you can store them in Mylar bags with an oxygen absorber. These bags are designed for longer-term storage and will be fine for 3–4 years. The only disadvantage to using Mylar bags is that they are not rodent proof. They are, however, great for earthquake zones.

CAN I USE ZIP-SEALABLE BAGS OR OTHER PLASTIC BAGS FOR THESE MEALS FOR LONG-TERM STORAGE?

Zip-sealable bags are not designed for long-term storage and are not recommended for repacking the freeze-dried meats and cheeses because they are too porous for these purposes. The only time I use zip-sealable bags is within the jars to keep some products separate for later use when I prepare meals. I also use them for short-term storage when I make mixes like the hamburger skillet meals (without freeze-dried meat!).

CAN I USE DEHYDRATED VEGETABLES IN THESE RECIPES INSTEAD OF FREEZE-DRIED ITEMS?

Not always. I use different products for different cooking times and applications. Generally freeze-dried products cook completely differently and use a lot less water to hydrate than dehydrated items.

CAN I USE MY OWN HOME-DEHYDRATED ITEMS?

Should you use dehydrated vegetables you made at home, you will have to adjust cooking times, amount of water needed, and how much of each vegetable you use in the recipes. I cannot promise you will have the same results.

HOW DO I PREPARE AND LABEL EACH MEAL?

With each individual jar, I clearly label contents and include the cooking directions. I also include the date the meal was made. This label can be printed and affixed with tape to the jar or written on the lid of the jar with permanent ink. In this way, I always know what is in each jar and how to prepare it. I also know the estimated shelf life of the meal. This will ensure that each meal is usable and identifiable. There's nothing worse than looking at a meal in a jar and wondering if it is supposed to end up as meat or cake!

CAN I USE ANOTHER BRAND OF FOOD STORAGE FOR THESE RECIPES?

Be aware that not all food storage is created equally! Some other companies use added sugars and preservatives and cut their products differently. Smaller or larger pieces of carrot, for example, will have different cooking times and use a different amount of liquid to hydrate. Generally, this will also affect the cooking time and quality of the finished recipes. In all cases, I am very product specific. The degree to which you follow my recipes is the degree to which you will have good results. I am, without fail, completely impressed with the consistent quality I find with Honeyville. These recipes use all Honeyville products for a reason: because they're outstanding! Honestly that's the reason I agreed to write this cookbook for them.

MEAL 1

COUNTRY-STYLE HAMBURGER STEW

- 1 cup Honeyville quick cook red beans
- 1 cup Honeyville freeze-dried mixed vegetables
- 1 cup Honeyville freeze-dried ground beef (or TVP beef)
- 1 cup Honeyville dehydrated diced potatoes
- ¼ cup Honeyville dehydrated onions
- ¼ cup Honeyville tomato powder
- 1 tsp. thyme
- 1 tsp. garlic
- ¼ cup flour
- 1 Tbsp. beef bouillon

Directions: Put beans, vegetables, ground beef, potatoes, and onions in a quart jar. Shake the tomato powder and seasonings into the jar. It will fit if you shake it really well. Top with an oxygen packet for longer-term storage (good on the shelf in a cool place up to 5–7 years), top with a new canning lid, and hand-tighten the metal ring.

Cooking directions: Remove oxygen packet and discard. In a gallon pot, combine stew mix with 6 cups water and bring to a boil. Reduce heat and simmer 20–30 minutes.

This is a great meal made completely out of food storage. It's amazing for camping or dinner any night of the week. It's perfect for giving to a sick neighbor or to someone you actually . . . like. I think my family likes it because the folks I cook for are down-home, raised-on-the-farm kind of people. They don't like a lot of green herbs and junk in their food (ironic isn't it?). Now and then I get "froofie" chef on them and roast some garlic or chop some tarragon, but for the most part we eat "regular people" food.

MEAL 2

TACO SOUP

1½ cups Honeyville quick cook red or black beans

1 cup Honeyville taco TVP

½ cup Honeyville dehydrated onion

⅓ cup Honeyville freeze-dried mixed peppers

¾ cup Honeyville freeze-dried corn

½ cup Honeyville tomato powder

1 Tbsp. homemade taco seasoning or Chef Tess Southwest Fajita seasoning

Directions: Put a funnel on the mouth of a quart jar and measure ingredients in the order above into the jar. When you get to the tomato powder, just shake the jar so it works its way into the cracks. Top with an oxygen packet for longer-term storage (good on the shelf in a cool place up to 5–7 years), top with a new canning lid, and hand-tighten the metal ring.

Cooking directions: Remove oxygen packet and discard. Place contents of jar in a gallon pot. Add 2 quarts (8 cups) water and simmer 20–30 minutes until veggies are tender. Serve with tortilla chips, sour cream, and salsa if desired.

This is a recipe I made from an old classic for taco soup. It's adapted using instant beans. Instead of taking hours to cook in a slow cooker, it takes just about 20 minutes! I'm super excited about it! Can you tell? It can fit conveniently in a quart-size jar, so it's perfect for food storage!

MEAL 3

DOUBLE CHEESEBURGER HAMBURGER SKILLET MEAL

- ½ cup Honeyville instant milk powder
- ½ cup Honeyville freeze-dried ground beef
- 2 cups Honeyville elbow macaroni or 227 g. dry pasta of your choice
- 3 Tbsp. cornstarch
- ¼ cup Honeyville freeze-dried onions
- ¼ cup Honeyville freeze-dried cheddar cheese
- ¼ cup blue cheese powder (optional)
- 1 tsp. beef bouillon (no MSG)
- ¼ tsp. turmeric

Directions: Put all ingredients in a quart jar. Top with an oxygen packet for longer-term storage (good on the shelf in a cool place up to 5–7 years), cover with a new canning lid, and hand-tighten the metal ring.

Cooking directions: Remove oxygen packet and discard. Combine contents of the jar in a large skillet with 6 cups hot water. Bring to a boil and cover. Simmer 12–15 minutes until noodles are tender. Sauce will thicken a little more as it cools.

MEAL 4

STROGANOFF SKILLET MEAL

½ cup Honeyville instant nonfat powdered milk

½ cup Honeyville sour cream powder

3 Tbsp. cornstarch

¼ cup Honeyville freeze-dried onion

1 tsp. beef bouillon

2 cups Honeyville elbow macaroni or shell macaroni

½ cup Honeyville freeze-dried ground beef

½ cup Honeyville freeze-dried mushrooms

1 Tbsp. golden balsamic vinegar powder

1 tsp. dehydrated minced garlic

⅛ tsp. nutmeg

⅛ tsp. pepper

3 Tbsp. Honeyville butter powder

Directions: Layer contents in a wide-mouth, quart-size jar, shaking the dry ingredients into the bulkier items. Top with an oxygen packet for longer-term storage (good on the shelf in a cool place up to 5–7 years), top with a new canning lid, and hand-tighten the metal ring.

Cooking directions: Remove oxygen packet and discard. Place contents of jar in a skillet. Add 6 cups water and bring to a boil over high heat. Reduce heat to a simmer and continue cooking for 12–15 minutes, stirring once or twice, but covering each time. When noodles are tender, season with additional salt and pepper if needed. Add more sour cream if desired as well.

This mix can easily be made for a convenience dinner as a "bag mix" and also as a meal in a jar. To make it for a "just add beef" meal, simply mix all the dry ingredients (except the meat). Put the mixture in a jar or zip-sealable bag. They are shelf stable as they sit in a zip-sealable bag for about 6 months. Cook a pound of beef in a deep pot. Add 5½ cups of water and simmer 12–15 minutes.

STROGANOFF SKILLET MEAL

CHEESE TURKEY NOODLE CASSEROLE

MEAL 5

CHEESE TURKEY NOODLE CASSEROLE

Put the following items in a quart jar (use a wide mouth funnel):

2 cups radiator or rotelli noodles

In a separate bag in the top of the jar, put

¼ cup Honeyville freeze-dried broccoli

½ cup Honeyville freeze-dried mixed vegetable mix

1 cup Honeyville freeze-dried turkey

½ cup Honeyville cheese sauce powder

¼ cup Honeyville freeze-dried diced celery

1 Tbsp. Honeyville freeze-dried onion

1½ tsp. Chef Tess All Purpose seasoning mix

Directions: Top with an oxygen packet for longer-term storage (good on the shelf in a cool place up to 5–7 years), top with a new canning lid, and hand-tighten the metal ring.

Cooking directions: Remove oxygen packet and discard. Carefully remove bag. Put contents of bag in a 2-quart saucepan with 2½ cups water and bring to a boil. Boil 5 minutes. Cover and turn off heat. While sauce is cooking, bring a gallon of water to a boil and cook pasta 10–12 minutes. When tender, drain. Stir into sauce mixture. Pour into casserole dish and top with additional cheese if desired.

MEAL 6

BROCCOLI CHEESE AND RICE CASSEROLE

Stir these 3 ingredients to combine and put in a quart jar (use a wide-mouth funnel):

- 2 cups Honeyville long grain rice
- 1 tsp. salt
- ¼ cup Honeyville dehydrated butter

In a separate bag on top of rice, place the following:

- ¼ cup Honeyville dehydrated celery
- ¼ cup Honeyville dehydrated onion
- 1 cup Honeyville freeze-dried broccoli
- 1 tsp. Chef Tess All Purpose seasoning mix
- ½ cup Honeyville cheese sauce powder
- ¼ cup Honeyville dehydrated butter powder

Directions: Seal bag. Top with an oxygen packet for longer-term storage (good on the shelf in a cool place up to 10–12 years), top with a new canning lid, and hand-tighten the metal ring.

Cooking directions: Remove oxygen packet and discard. Open bag, carefully ease contents into a quart saucepan, and add 2 cups water. Bring

to a boil and reduce heat. Simmer 5–6 minutes. Turn off heat and let sit 5–6 minutes. While the sauce is cooking, place the rice in a quart-size pot with a tight-fitting lid. Add 4 cups boiling water or chicken stock. Cook on lowest heat 17–20 minutes, covered, until rice is tender. Spoon broccoli cheese sauce over rice and enjoy.

MEAL 7

TURKEY NOODLE SKILLET MEAL

Put the following items in a quart jar (use a wide-mouth funnel):

- 2 cups Honeyville egg noodles
- ½ cup Honeyville freeze-dried vegetable mix
- ⅓ cup Honeyville cheese sauce powder
- ⅓ cup Honeyville powdered milk
- ¼ cup Honeyville dehydrated butter
- 1 cup Honeyville freeze-dried turkey chunks
- ½ cup Honeyville freeze-dried mushroom slices
- 1 Tbsp. dehydrated onions
- 1 tsp. Chef Tess Romantic Italian seasoning

Directions: Top with an oxygen packet for longer-term storage (good on the shelf in a cool place up to 5–7 years), top with a new canning lid, and hand-tighten the metal ring.

Cooking directions: Remove oxygen packet and discard. In a large skillet, combine contents of jar with 3½ cups hot water over high heat and bring to a boil. Reduce heat and simmer 10–12 minutes, stirring every few minutes. Turn off heat and let sit 3–5 minutes. Sauce will thicken as it sits.

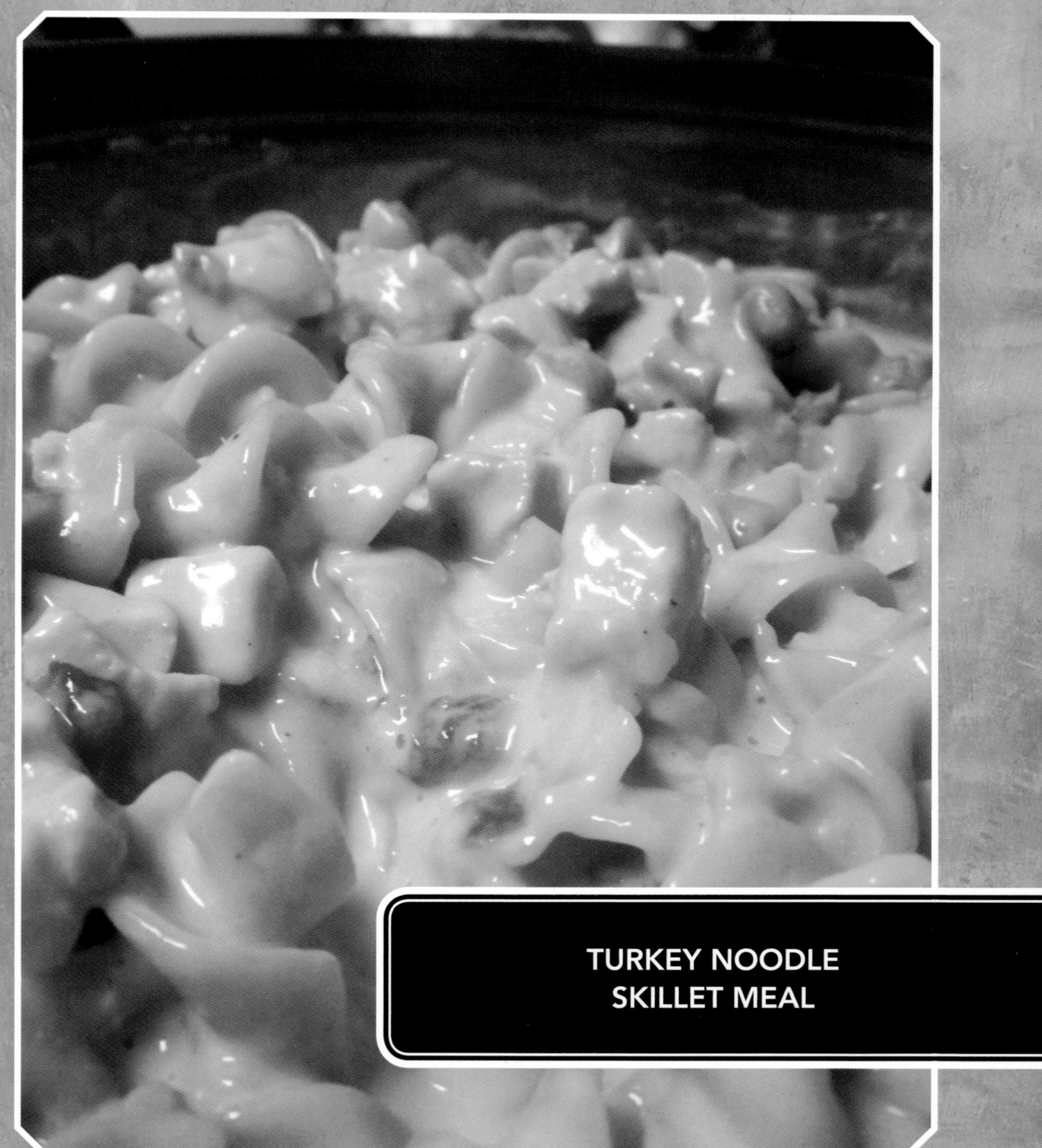

TURKEY NOODLE SKILLET MEAL

SAUCY "BAKED" ZITI WITH SAUSAGE AND MUSHROOMS

MEAL 8

SAUCY "BAKED" ZITI WITH SAUSAGE AND MUSHROOMS

Put the following items in a quart jar (use a wide mouth funnel):

- 2/3 cup Honeyville tomato powder
- 1/3 cup Honeyville dehydrated onion
- 1 Tbsp. Chef Tess Romantic Italian seasoning
- 1/3 cup Honeyville freeze-dried sausage or sausage TVP
- 2/3 cup Honeyville freeze–dried ground beef or beef TVP
- 1 cup ziti noodles (3 oz.)
- 1/3 cup Honeyville freeze-dried mushrooms
- 2/3 cup Honeyville freeze-dried mozzarella cheese (in a snack baggie)

Directions: Top with an oxygen packet for longer-term storage (good on the shelf in a cool place up to 5–7 years), cover with a new canning lid, and hand-tighten the metal ring.

Cooking directions: Remove oxygen packet and discard. Place contents of jar (except for cheese) in a covered skillet or pot with 4½ cups water. Simmer 15–20 minutes until pasta is tender and sauce is thick. (For solar oven: 30–40 minutes, covered.) Place cheese in a bowl and spray lightly with water. Let sit for 5 minutes. Uncover cooked pasta mixture. Top with cheese. Cover again and allow cheese to melt, about 5 minutes.

MEAL 9

BEEFY TACO RICE

Put the following items in a quart jar (use a wide-mouth funnel):

- ½ cup Honeyville freeze-dried ground beef or beef TVP
- 1½ cups Honeyville parboiled rice
- ½ cup Honeyville freeze-dried bell pepper
- ½ cup Honeyville dehydrated onion
- 1 Tbsp. Chef Tess Southwest Fajita seasoning
- 1 tsp. dehydrated minced garlic
- 1 Tbsp. dehydrated minced ancho chilies
- 1½ tsp. salt
- ½ tsp. smoked paprika
- ¼ cup Honeyville tomato powder
- 1 bay leaf
- 2 tsp. beef bouillon

Directions: Top with an oxygen packet for longer-term storage (good on the shelf in a cool place up to 5–7 years). Cover with a new canning lid and hand-tighten the metal ring.

Cooking directions: Remove oxygen packet and discard. Add contents of jar to 5½ cups boiling water. Cover and simmer on low 25–30 minutes until tender. Top with cheese or sour cream if desired.

MEAL 10

BEAN AND RICE FAJITA CASSEROLE

Put the following items in a quart jar (use a wide-mouth funnel):

- 2 cups Honeyville quick cook red or black beans
- 1 cup long grain rice
- ½ cup Honeyville freeze-dried bell pepper
- ½ cup Honeyville dehydrated onion
- 1 Tbsp. Chef Tess All Purpose seasoning
- ½ tsp. cumin seed
- ½ tsp. oregano leaves (or 1 drop oil of oregano)
- 1 tsp. minced garlic
- 1 bay leaf
- ½ cup Honeyville cheese sauce powder
- ¼ cup Honeyville tomato powder

Directions: Top with an oxygen packet for longer-term storage (good on the shelf in a cool place up to 5–7 years), top with a new canning lid and hand-tighten the metal ring.

Cooking directions: Remove oxygen packet and discard. Preheat oven to 350 degrees. Place contents of jar in a deep, covered casserole dish and add 6 cups very hot water. Place, covered, in conventional oven and bake for 30–35 minutes.

Mea

MEAL 11

GOLDEN POTATO, CHEESE, AND SAUSAGE CASSEROLE

Put the following items in a quart jar (use a wide-mouth funnel):

- 1 cup Honeyville cheese sauce mix
- ½ cup Honeyville dehydrated sour cream
- ⅓ cup Honeyville dehydrated onion
- 1½ tsp. dehydrated minced garlic
- 1 cup Honeyville freeze-dried sausage (or ham)
- 2 cups (4 oz.) Honeyville dehydrated hash brown potatoes
- ⅛ tsp. ground nutmeg
- ½ tsp. cracked fresh pepper
- 1 bay leaf

Directions: Top with an oxygen packet for longer-term storage (good on the shelf in a cool place up to 5–7 years). Cover with a new canning lid and hand-tighten the metal ring.

Cooking directions: Remove oxygen packet and discard. Preheat oven to 350 degrees. Combine contents in a deep casserole dish with 5½ cups hot water. Cover 10 minutes. Bake in oven 1 hour, covered, or in the microwave on high 15 minutes, uncovered. You may top with additional cheese, crushed corn flakes, or crushed crackers if desired.

GOLDEN POTATO, CHEESE, AND SAUSAGE CASSEROLE

MEAL 12

CREAMY CHICKEN VEGGIE CASSEROLE

Put the following items in a quart jar (use a wide-mouth funnel):

- 1¾ cups wide egg noodles
- ½ cup Honeyville freeze-dried vegetable mix
- 1 cup Honeyville freeze-dried chicken chunks
- ½ cup Honeyville freeze-dried peas
- ¼ cup Honeyville freeze-dried mushroom slices
- 2 Tbsp. Honeyville dehydrated onions
- 1 tsp. Chef Tess Romantic Italian seasoning
- ½ cup Honeyville cheese sauce powder
- ⅓ cup Honeyville powdered milk
- ⅓ cup Honeyville powdered sour cream
- ¼ cup Honeyville dehydrated butter

Directions: Top with an oxygen packet for longer-term storage (good on the shelf in a cool place up to 5 years). Cover with a new canning lid and hand-tighten the metal ring.

Cooking directions: Remove oxygen packet and discard. In a casserole dish, combine the entire contents of the jar with 4 cups hot water. Let sit 5 minutes. Cover and bake in solar oven at 350 degrees for 30–35 minutes or in microwave in covered deep casserole dish for 15 minutes.

BONUS: Bread crumb topping

While the casserole is baking, I make bread crumb topping. This is optional but adds a lot of texture and flavor. I prefer, when cooking with the solar oven, to do the topping on a separate burner or, if microwaving, cooking the topping on the stove to crisp it. This saves a lot of time and, with the solar cooker, gets a crispy topping I can't normally get. I use homemade 9-grain ciabatta. Put a few pieces in a food processor or finely grind in a hand-powered processor. Add 2 Tbsp. olive oil, ½ cup of the crumbs, and ½ tsp. of my Romantic Italian seasoning. Put the crumbs in a hot skillet and stir until toasted.

MEAL 13

YANKEE POT ROAST BEEF AND GRAVY OVER GARLIC MASHED POTATOES

Gravy:

- 2 cups Honeyville freeze-dried diced beef
- ¼ cup Ultra Gel or cornstarch
- ¼ cup Honeyville freeze-dried mushrooms
- ⅓ cup Honeyville dehydrated onion
- 2 tsp. beef bouillon
- 1 tsp. dehydrated minced garlic
- 1 tsp. Chef Tess All Purpose seasoning
- 1 Tbsp. Honeyville tomato powder

Mashed potatoes:

- 1½ cups Honeyville potato flakes
- 1 tsp. granulated garlic
- 3 Tbsp. Honeyville powdered butter

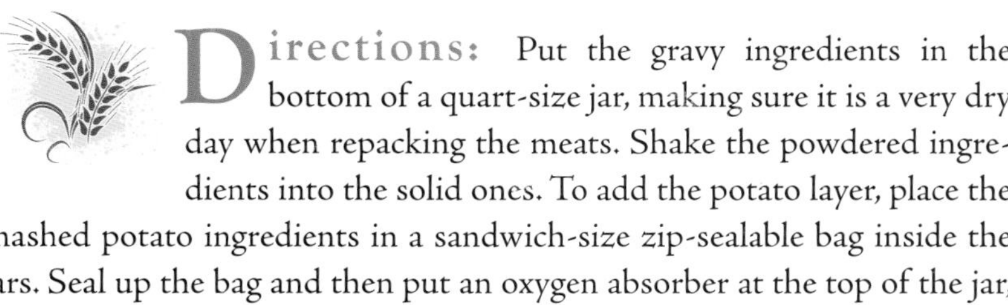

Directions: Put the gravy ingredients in the bottom of a quart-size jar, making sure it is a very dry day when repacking the meats. Shake the powdered ingredients into the solid ones. To add the potato layer, place the mashed potato ingredients in a sandwich-size zip-sealable bag inside the jars. Seal up the bag and then put an oxygen absorber at the top of the jar, being sure it is inside the jar and not at all on the rim. If this is kept in a cool, dry place, it will have a shelf life of up to 10 years.

Cooking directions: Remove oxygen packet and discard. Carefully remove the bag of potato pearls by opening the bag, emptying a little into a 2-quart metal bowl, and then easing the baggie out of the jar. Pour the entire contents of the potato baggie into the bowl. Pour the gravy mixture into a 2-quart pot. Add 4 cups very hot water to the gravy mix. Whisk well. Place on stove and bring to a simmer 15–20 minutes. Turn off heat and leave covered 5 additional minutes. While the gravy sits, bring 2 cups water to a boil in a separate pan. Then pour into the potatoes, stirring well.

I think the ultimate sweet and savory combination has got to be sausage and corn. The first time I tasted Honeyville freeze-dried corn, I was transported by its sweet flavor, in my mind, to my childhood. Dad would grow corn in the family garden, and many times I could be found hiding in the tall stalks, sitting in the dirt, with my cute little-girl hands wrapped around a freshly shucked corn cob. I loved that sweet flavor.

MEAL 14

SOUTHERN-STYLE CREAMED CORN AND SAUSAGE

In a quart-size jar, combine the following:

- ¼ cup Honeyville powdered butter
- ½ tsp. salt
- ½ tsp. Chef Tess Romantic Italian seasoning
- 1 Tbsp. Honeyville granulated honey
- 2 Tbsp. Honeyville corn masa (or cornmeal works)
- ½ cup Honeyville sour cream powder
- 2 Tbsp. Honeyville dehydrated green onions
- fresh-ground black pepper
- 3 cups Honeyville freeze-dried corn
- ¼ cup Honeyville freeze-dried sausage or TVP sausage

Directions: Shake dry ingredients into the corn and sausage. Top with an oxygen absorber for longer-term storage (good on the shelf in a cool place up to 5–7 years). Seal with a new canning lid.

Cooking directions: Remove oxygen packet and discard. Combine all ingredients in a medium heavy pot. Add 4 cups hot water and stir over medium heat until cooked through and tender, about 20 minutes.

MEAL 15

DALLAS-STYLE CHICKEN NOODLE SOUP

In a pint-size jar, combine the following:

½ cup freeze-dried chicken or chicken-flavored TVP

1½ cups broken linguine or fettuccine noodles (I go by weight—3.5 oz.)

1 Tbsp. plus 1 tsp. chicken bouillon (no MSG and low sodium is best)

1 tsp. garlic granules or powder

¼ tsp. dry thyme

¼ tsp. Chef Tess All Purpose seasoning mix

⅛ tsp. turmeric (for color and flavor)

Directions: Top the jar with one oxygen absorber and seal jar tightly. This meal is good on the shelf in a cool, dry place up to 10 years.

Cooking directions: Remove oxygen packet and discard. Combine contents of the jar with 5 cups boiling water. Simmer 12–15 minutes until noodles and chicken are tender. Serve hot.

This meal was a request from a friend named Dallas at the Honeyville retail store in Arizona. It has nothing to do with anything actually in Dallas, Texas. Sorry, Texas. As for Dallas, she loves chicken noodle soup but, as she put it, "without all the vegetables and big herbs and stuff in there." I love her. A great reminder that though I may be creating some remarkable gourmet jar meals that span international cuisine, there's also a need for some basic meals that every family in the good ol' United States of America will eat. This meal is made in a pint-size jar. Make sure you have the smaller jars on hand.

MEAL 16

CLASSIC CHILI

2 cups Honeyville quick cook red or black beans

1 cup Honeyville tomato powder (shake down into the beans or everything won't fit in the jar)

1 cup Honeyville freeze-dried diced beef or chili TVP

½ cup Honeyville dehydrated onion

½ cup Honeyville freeze-dried bell peppers

¼ cup Honeyville freeze-dried celery

1 Tbsp. beef bouillon (no MSG)

1 Tbsp. chili powder (more or less, depending on how you like your chili)

1 Tbsp. Chef Tess All Purpose seasoning

1 tsp. hot chili flakes (if you like it hot)

Directions: Pack the ingredients as tightly as possible in a quart jar. Top with an oxygen absorber. This meal is good on the shelf in a cool, dry place up to 10 years.

Cooking directions: Remove oxygen packet and discard. Combine the contents of the jar with 7–8 cups hot water (depending on how thick you like your chili) and simmer over medium-high heat 25–30 minutes until hydrated and ready to eat. Serve with hydrated, freeze-dried cheese if desired or just have it plain in all its glory.

This is a classic chili. Some like it hot. Some like it mild. But 99 percent of the people I know will eat it at least twice a month . . . if not more.

MEAL 17

HAWAIIAN-STYLE TERIYAKI BEEF AND VEGETABLES WITH RICE

1 cup Honeyville freeze-dried diced beef

1 cup Honeyville freeze-dried broccoli

¾ cup Honeyville freeze-dried bell pepper

¼ cup Honeyville freeze-dried onion or dehydrated green onion

1 pkg. (1.5-oz.) NOH of Hawaii Teri-burger meatloaf seasoning mix

2 Tbsp. Ultra Gel (modified cornstarch) (Note: 2 Tbsp. regular cornstarch will work, but you must boil the sauce)

1 cup Honeyville long grain or parboiled rice

Directions: In a wide mouth quart jar, layer beef, broccoli, bell pepper, and onion. Shake the seasoning mix and the Ultra Gel or cornstarch into the meat and veggies. Put rice in a baggie on top of the veggie mixture. Top with an oxygen absorber for long-term storage. This meal will be shelf stable 7–10 years.

Cooking directions: Remove oxygen packet and discard. Combine rice with 2 cups boiling water in a medium saucepan with a tight-fitting lid. When rice and water come to a boil, reduce heat to very low and simmer 20 minutes. For sauce: Combine the meat and veggie mixture at the bottom of the jar with 3½ cups very hot water in a pan. Allow to sit 10 minutes to absorb water. Place on stove and turn on medium heat, cooking 5–7 minutes more until sauce has slightly thickened. The rice and sauce will be finished cooking at about the same time if you cook them simultaneously.

MEAL 18

POLYNESIAN SWEET AND SOUR CHICKEN BAKED BEANS

- 2 cups Honeyville quick cook red beans
- 1 cup Honeyville freeze-dried chicken or chicken TVP
- ¼ cup Honeyville dehydrated onion
- ½ cup NOH teriyaki powder
- 2 Tbsp. golden balsamic vinegar powder
- ¼ cup Honeyville granulated honey
- 1 Tbsp. dehydrated minced garlic
- 2 Tbsp. Ultra Gel or cornstarch
- ½ cup Honeyville freeze-dried bell peppers
- ½ cup Honeyville freeze-dried pineapple

Directions: Put ingredients in a wide-mouth quart jar, shaking the powdered ingredients in before adding the bell peppers and pineapple. Top with an oxygen absorber and a new canning lid. This meal will be shelf-stable up to 10 years.

Cooking directions: Remove oxygen packet and discard. Add 5 cups water and simmer on low for 30 minutes.

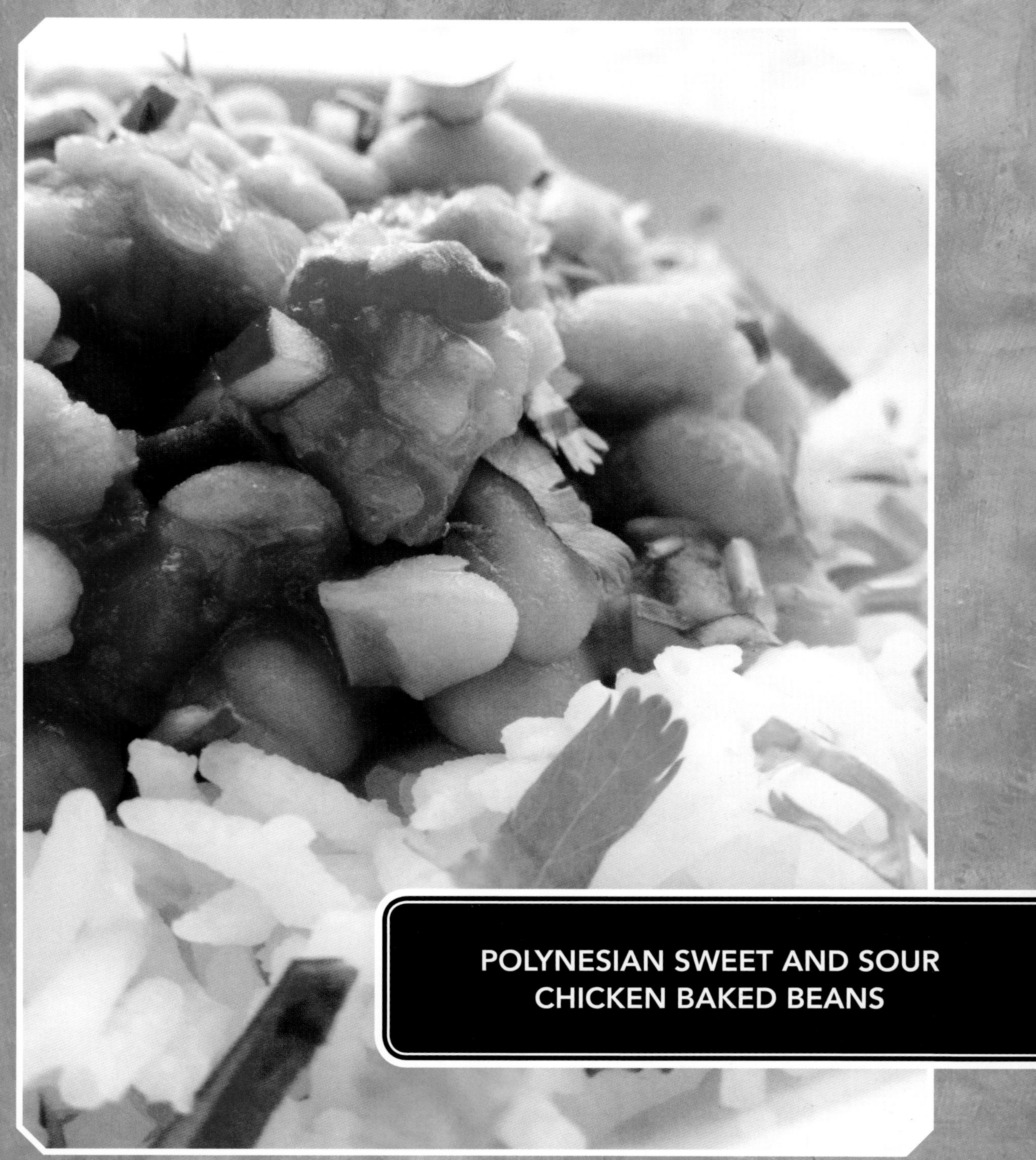

POLYNESIAN SWEET AND SOUR CHICKEN BAKED BEANS

6-GRAIN CARROT CAKE BREAKFAST PUDDING

BREAKFAST 1

6-GRAIN CARROT CAKE BREAKFAST PUDDING

½ cup Honeyville freeze-dried pineapple or freeze-dried apples

1 cup Honeyville dehydrated carrots

½ cup instant nonfat powdered milk

¼ cup Honeyville powdered butter

½ cup Honeyville granulated honey or sugar

2 tsp. coconut powder flavoring (optional)

1 Tbsp. vanilla powder flavoring (optional)

2 Tbsp. Honeyville instant vanilla pudding mix

½ tsp. salt

1 tsp. Chef Tess Wise Woman of the East spice blend

2 cups Honeyville 6-grain rolled cereal

Directions: Place pineapple and carrots in a quart jar. Top with powdered milk, butter, honey, optional flavorings, pudding mix, salt, and spice blend. Shake the dry ingredients down into the carrots and pineapple. Top with 6-grain cereal. The jar will be full. Top with oxygen absorber. This meal will be shelf stable up to 5 years.

Cooking directions: Remove oxygen packet and discard. Bring 5 cups water to a rolling boil. Add contents of the jar to the water and stir. Lower heat to a simmer and cook 10–12 minutes. Turn off heat. Cover and let sit 5 minutes (to be sure pineapple is hydrated). Serve warm. Drizzle with milk, honey, or syrup and top with chopped pecans or any nuts if desired.

My grandmother used to make the most amazing old-fashioned carrot pudding for Thanksgiving. This breakfast cereal tastes like a cross between her pudding and a rich carrot cake. It's not as sweet as carrot cake or as dense as grandma's pudding, so add more sweetener if you prefer. I just drizzle this with some coconut milk and top it with toasted nuts. However you do it, this is going to be a family favorite. I know it will be.

SWEET POTATO AND CORN SKILLET FRITTATA

½ cup Honeyville freeze-dried sausage

1 cup Honeyville freeze-dried sweet potato

½ cup Honeyville freeze-dried corn

½ cup Honeyville freeze-dried mushrooms

½ cup Honeyville freeze-dried bell pepper

¼ cup Honeyville dehydrated onion

12 scoops (equal to 9 eggs) Ova Easy egg crystals (1.3 oz.)

1 cup Honeyville freeze-dried Colby cheese

1 tsp. Chef Tess Southwest Fajita seasoning

½ tsp. dry oregano

½ tsp. fresh cracked pepper or ancho chile powder

2 Tbsp. Honeyville all-purpose flour

2 Tbsp. Honeyville instant nonfat powdered milk

1 Tbsp. Honeyville sour cream powder

Directions: Put the sausage and veggies in the bottom of a quart jar and top with the eggs. Shake the eggs down into the cracks. Add the cheese and the remaining dry ingredients. Top with oxygen absorber. This meal is shelf-stable up to 5 years.

Cooking directions: Remove oxygen packet and discard. Combine 3 cups cool water and the contents of the jar in a 2-quart bowl and allow

to hydrate about 10 minutes. Whisk a couple of times after 5 minutes to be sure everything gets moist. Lightly oil a 10-inch skillet with a tightly fitting lid (or your solar oven casserole pan). Heat skillet on low for 2 or 3 minutes. Pour in egg mixture. Cover with tightly fitting lid and allow to cook 15–17 minutes on very low. Do not uncover. If you are using your solar oven, it will take 20–25 minutes at 350 degrees. Turn off heat. Do not uncover. Allow to carryover-cook another 5–7 minutes, covered. Remove lid and slice as you would a pizza. Serve warm with salsa of your choice.

BREAKFAST 3

SPICED MAPLE PEACHES AND CREAM RICE PUDDING

1 cup long grain rice

1 cup instant nonfat powdered milk

½ cup Honeyville peaches and cream smoothie mix

1 cup Honeyville freeze-dried peaches

2 tsp. powdered maple flavoring (optional)

½ cup Honeyville instant vanilla pudding

Directions: Place all ingredients in a quart jar. Top with an oxygen absorber. This meal is shelf stable up to 5 years.

Cooking directions: Remove oxygen packet and discard. Combine with 5 cups hot water. Bring to a boil. Reduce to a low simmer and cover with a tight lid. Simmer 25–30 minutes, stirring every 5 minutes. Take off the heat and allow to sit 5–10 minutes longer. This can be placed in a solar oven in a gallon-size container with a tight-fitting lid. Bake 1 hour at 350 degrees, stirring every 20 minutes.

BREAKFAST 4

MY MOM'S HAM AND ZUCCHINI QUICHE CASSEROLE

- 2 Tbsp. Honeyville dehydrated green onions
- 1 cup Honeyville freeze-dried ham
- ½ cup Honeyville freeze-dried zucchini
- ½ cup Honeyville freeze-dried bell peppers
- 1 Tbsp. Honeyville powdered butter
- ¼ cup Ova Easy egg crystals (no substitutions)
- ½ cup Honeyville powdered sour cream
- 2 Tbsp. Ultra Gel
- ½ tsp. Chef Tess Romantic Italian seasoning
- 1 cup Honeyville freeze-dried cheddar cheese

Directions: Put the green onion, ham, zucchini, and bell peppers in a quart jar. Add the powdered ingredients and shake them down into the veggie mixture. Add the cheese and top with an oxygen absorber. This meal is shelf-stable up to 5 years.

Cooking directions: Remove oxygen packet and discard. Preheat oven to 325 degrees. Pour the jar ingredients in a 2-quart bowl and add 2½ cups cool water. Allow to hydrate 10 minutes. Lightly grease a 9 × 9 casserole dish (or solar oven 9-inch round pan works too). Cover with foil. Bake until set, about 50 minutes. Do not overbake. May be stored in refrigerator after baking and heated for service.

BREAKFAST 5

COUNTRY SAUSAGE, HASH BROWN, AND PEPPER-CHEESE SCRAMBLED EGG BREAKFAST SKILLET

- 2 cups Honeyville dehydrated diced potatoes
- 1 cup Honeyville freeze-dried sausage (no substitutions)
- 1 tsp. Chef Tess All Purpose seasoning mix
- ⅓ cup Ova Easy egg crystals (no substitutions)
- ⅓ cup Honeyville freeze-dried cheddar cheese
- ⅓ cup Honeyville freeze-dried bell peppers
- 2 Tbsp. Honeyville freeze-dried mushrooms
- ½ tsp. Chef Tess Romantic Italian seasoning

Directions: Place the potatoes, sausage, and All Purpose seasoning in a wide-mouth quart jar. In a small zip-sealable baggie on top of the potatoes, sausage, and seasoning, place the egg crystals, cheese, bell peppers, mushrooms, and Romantic Italian seasoning. Seal bag. Top the jar with oxygen absorber. This meal is shelf-stable up to 10 years.

Cooking directions: Remove oxygen packet and discard. In a large, 12-inch, nonstick skillet, combine the potatoes, sausage, and All Purpose seasoning with 4 cups boiling water. Cover and allow to hydrate 10–15 minutes until potatoes are tender. In a quart-size bowl, combine the contents of the baggie with ⅔ cup cool water, whisking well. Allow to hydrate

5 minutes. Drain any extra water once the potatoes are tender. The fat from the sausage will keep the potatoes from sticking to the pan. Cook 10–15 minutes over medium heat, stirring once or twice but allowing the potatoes to brown well. In a separate small, nonstick skillet on low heat, slowly cook the egg mixture, stirring often. Serve eggs over the potato mixture.

BREAKFAST 6

SPICED SAMOAN COCONUT-CREAM FARINA WITH MANGO

In a pint jar, place the following:

- 1 cup Honeyville farina
- 1/3 cup Honeyville Tropical Monsoon smoothie mix
- 1/3 cup Honeyville granulated honey
- 1/3 cup Honeyville freeze-dried mango
- 1 tsp. pineapple flavor powder
- ½ tsp. Chef Tess Wise Woman of the East spice blend

Directions: Top the jar with an oxygen absorber. This meal is shelf-stable up to 5 years.

Cooking directions: Remove oxygen packet and discard. Combine contents of jar with 4 cups boiling water, whisking briskly until combined. Simmer 3–4 minutes and serve hot with toasted coconut if desired.

BREAKFAST 7

CARAMEL RASPBERRY CHOCOLATE TRUFFLE BREAKFAST PUDDING

In a pint jar, place the following:

- 1 cup Honeyville farina
- ¼ cup Honeyville chocolate raspberry hot cocoa mix
- ¼ cup dark baking cocoa powder (Dutch)
- ⅓ cup Honeyville freeze-dried raspberries
- 1½ tsp. butterscotch flavor powder
- ⅓ cup Honeyville granulated honey or sugar

Directions: Top the jar with an oxygen absorber. This meal is shelf-stable up to 5 years.

Cooking directions: Remove oxygen packet and discard. Combine contents with 4 cups rapidly boiling water, whisking briskly. Simmer on low 3–4 minutes. Serve hot with chocolate chips if desired.

SIDE DISHES

INSTANT CHEESY BROCCOLI RICE

2 cups instant rice

1 cup Honeyville broccoli cheese soup mix

½ cup Honeyville cheese sauce powder

2 tsp. onion powder

¼ tsp. black pepper

4 cups water

Directions: Combine dry ingredients. Bring water to a boil in a half-gallon pan with a tight-fitting lid. Add the dry ingredients and whisk well. Stir about 2 minutes, returning to a boil. Cover. Turn off heat. Allow to sit 10 minutes until rice is hydrated and water is absorbed.

This is a great side dish that works just like those packets of "instant" broccoli cheese rice that you get at the grocery store . . . but you can make it at home and control the ingredients! How cool is that?

CRANBERRY MIXED BERRY RELISH

- 2 cups Honeyville dried cranberries
- 1 cup Honeyville dried cherries
- ½ cup Honeyville freeze-dried raspberries
- 2 Tbsp. Ultra Gel
- 2 Tbsp. Honeyville lemonade powder
- 1 Tbsp. dehydrated orange zest (or 2 Tbsp. fresh orange zest)
- ¼ tsp. Chef Tess Wise Woman of the East spice blend
- 3 cups water

Directions: Simmer all ingredients over medium-high heat in a quart-size pot, stirring occasionally, 7–10 minutes until berries absorb water and sauce becomes slightly thick. Turn off heat and allow to sit 10 minutes more. Transfer sauce to a dish and put in the fridge. Allow to set 3–4 hours or overnight. Serve well chilled as a relish for roasted chicken, turkey, and beef.

We love this on Thanksgiving . . . and almost anytime with chicken or turkey. It's got just the right balance of sweet and savory and makes a great addition to your meals. Try it with your next roasted chicken. It is delicious on turkey sandwiches and turkey burgers as well.

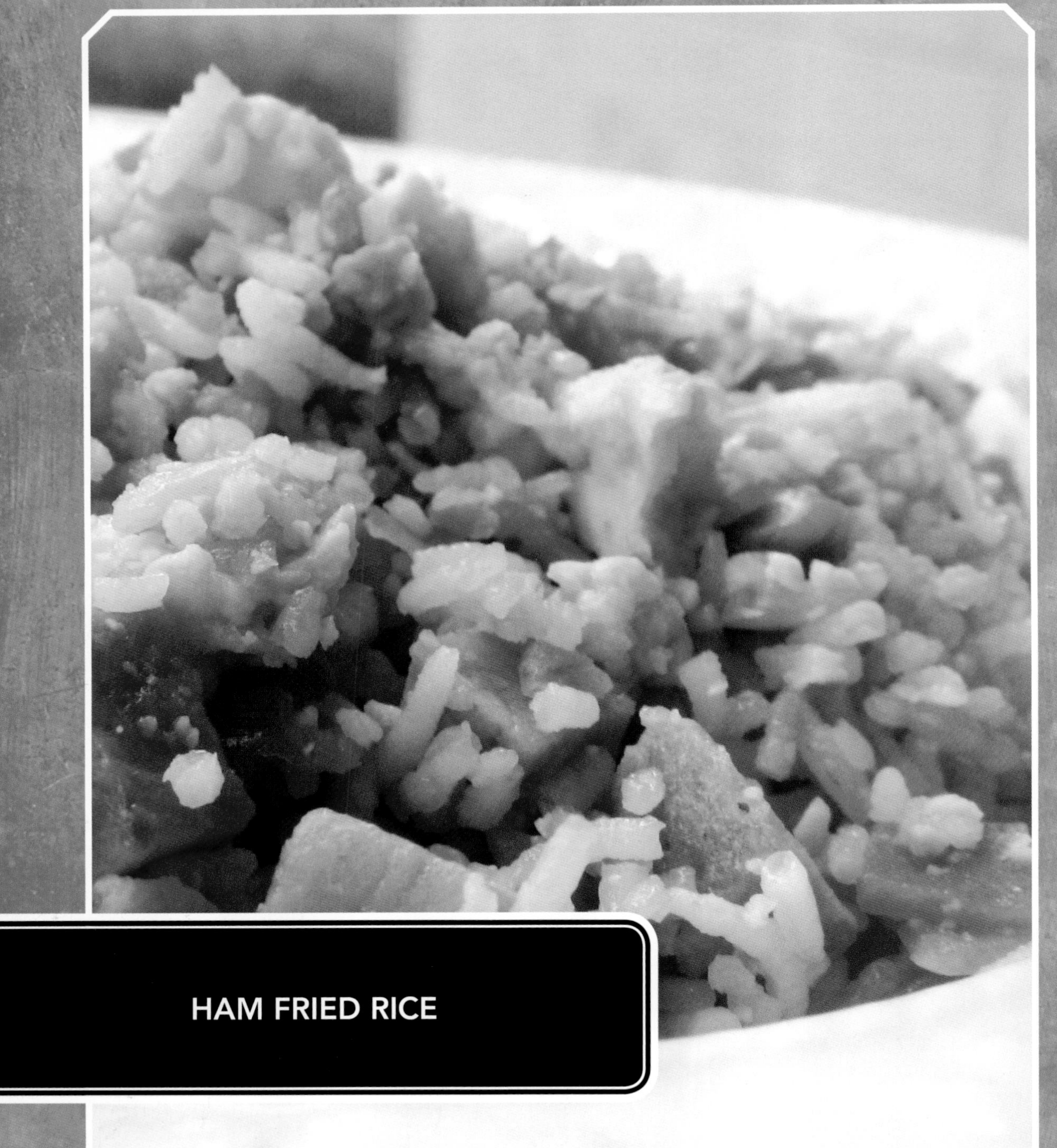

HAM FRIED RICE

HAM FRIED RICE

¼ cup Honeyville dehydrated carrot dices

½ cup Honeyville freeze-dried green peas

¼ cup Honeyville dehydrated chopped onions

1 cup Honeyville freeze-dried ham

4 cups water

1 Tbsp. sesame oil

4 cups cooked Honeyville white or brown rice, cold (after cooking measurement)

½ cup Honeyville freeze-dried scrambled eggs, hydrated

3 Tbsp. soy sauce

Directions: In a quart-size pot, combine carrots, green peas, onions, and ham with water. Bring to a boil over high heat. Lower the heat and simmer for 10 minutes or until vegetables and meat are reconstituted and tender. Drain and set aside. Heat a frying pan or wok over medium-high heat. Add sesame oil to the pan or wok, swirling to coat. Add rice, along with the ham and vegetable mixture, and stir-fry for 2 minutes until everything is heated through. Stir in egg and soy sauce gently.

What is it about American Chinese food that makes me so happy? I think you'll be pleasantly surprised to find that you can make this classic fried rice using all your food storage . . . even the meat! It's one of my family's favorites.

BASIC GRAVY MIX

- ½ cup all-purpose flour
- 3 Tbsp. beef or chicken bouillon granules, MSG free
- 2 Tbsp. onion powder
- 1 Tbsp. garlic powder (not granules or it will be too strong)
- ½ tsp. ground celery seed
- ½ tsp. black pepper
- 1 tsp. ground thyme
- 1 bay leaf

Directions: Place all ingredients in a half-pint sealable jar. Repeat as needed for however many mixes you want to make. Please note, this mix makes 8 cups gravy.

To make: Whisk mix with 2 cups milk or water . When smooth, add 6 more cups of milk or water. Simmer over medium heat, stirring occasionally, 10–15 minutes.

Smaller batches: ¼ cup mix yields 2 cups gravy. Divide among 4 snack-size baggies and provide 1 bay leaf per bag.

How much do you pay for a packet of gravy mix from the grocery store, only to find that it's loaded with added chemicals and products you don't want? The flavor of this homemade gravy mix is amazing, and the cost is pennies! Plus it ends up as light, delightful gravy. This recipe makes light, thin gravy perfect to coat the back of a spoon but not be a pudding on your potatoes. If you prefer thicker gravy, double the flour or cornstarch.

BASIC GLUTEN-FREE GRAVY MIX

¼ cup cornstarch or ⅓ cup Ultra Gel

1 Tbsp. plus 1 tsp. beef or chicken stock granules, MSG free if you prefer (make sure it's labeled gluten-free)

1 Tbsp. onion powder or freeze-dried onions

1 tsp. Chef Tess All Purpose seasoning mix

1 bay leaf

Directions: Place all ingredients in a half-pint sealable jar. Repeat as needed for however many mixes you want to make. Please note, this mix makes 4 cups gravy.

To make: Whisk mix with 4 cups milk or water (broth or stock if you omit the bouillon). Simmer over medium heat, stirring occasionally, 10–15 minutes.

Smaller Batch:

2 Tbsp. cornstarch or 3 Tbsp. Ultra Gel

2 tsp. beef or chicken stock granules (Shirley J brand is one of my favorite)

1 tsp. onion powder

¼ tsp. Chef Tess All Purpose seasoning mix

Whisk mix with 2 cups stock or milk in a medium saucepan with a heavy bottom. Simmer over medium heat 5 minutes for cornstarch sauces, 10–15 minutes if you use flour.

Yields 2 cups.

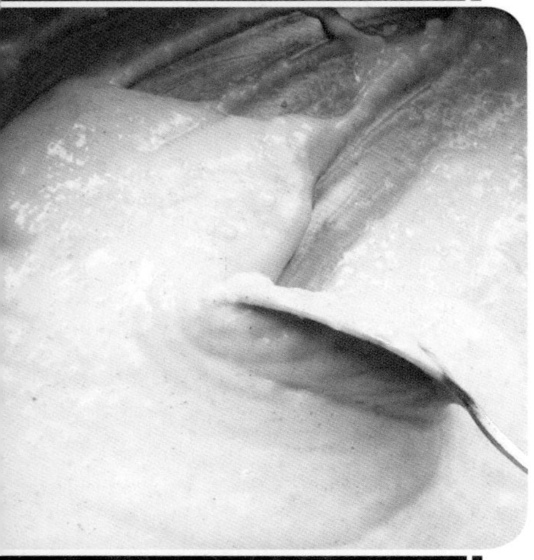

CONDENSED SOUP REPLACEMENT MIX

¼ cup cornstarch or ⅓ cup Ultra Gel

2 tsp. chicken bouillon/stock granules (usually I use Shirley J brand)

1 Tbsp. Honeyville freeze-dried onions

¼ cup Honeyville instant nonfat powdered milk

2 Tbsp. Honeyville sour cream powder

½ tsp. Chef Tess All Purpose seasoning mix

Directions: To cook, combine mix with 1¼ cups water, whisking over medium heat. Heat until thick, about 5 minutes. It will thicken more as it cools, so don't add a lot of extra thickener or you'll end up with glue. Yes, it does weigh just about the same amount as the contents of one small can of cream-o-gunk soup, give or take half an ounce. I'm not worried. If you use Ultra Gel, you can skip the cooking step and just combine the full mix with warm water using a wire whisk. It will thicken in about 5 minutes. Yes, you did just make instant condensed soup pudding. Mmm. Pudding pie.

For convenient mixes: Put a single batch in a snack-size sealable bag. Expel as much air as possible and put up to 4 baggies in a quart-size, wide-mouth jar. This is a fantastic way to have not only the equivalent of one can of condensed soup, but also an easy grab when you have a recipe that calls for condensed soup. Just pull out a baggie. I don't even write cooking directions on the baggies. I simply write how much water to add on the top of the jar. I double the recipe and know that each baggie will make 2 cans of soup. The quart-size jar stuffed with baggies makes the equivalent of 10 cans of soup. Each mix (using cornstarch) costs about 7 cents. Yes. 10 cans' worth of soup for 70 cents. That's a whole lot less than 10 dollars for 10 cans.

How many recipes do you have that start with a can of condensed cream of mushroom soup? How about cutting that expense from your family food budget and making your own convenient mix? This is easy, delicious, and so budget friendly!

To make cream of mushroom: Crush ¼ cup Honeyville freeze-dried mushrooms down to 2 tablespoons. Add to your mix.

To make cream of celery: Add 2 tablespoons Honeyville freeze-dried celery to the mix.

Note: Cornstarch will lose its ability to thicken once frozen. Opt for Ultra Gel for freezer sauces.

CLASSIC PEA SALAD

3 cups Honeyville freeze-dried peas

½ cup Honeyville freeze-dried cheddar cheese

¼ cup Honeyville dehydrated green onions

¼ cup Honeyville freeze-dried bell peppers (crushed)

½ tsp. fresh cracked black pepper

¼ tsp. dill

¼ tsp. garlic powder

¼ tsp. salt

¼ tsp. pepper

1 Tbsp. Honeyville lemonade powder

½ cup mayonnaise or olive oil

Directions: Hydrate peas with 3 cups warm water 10–15 minutes until revived. Add remaining ingredients to the peas. Stir and refrigerate 1 hour. Serve well chilled.

This is my classic refreshing summer salad, and it is a fabulous addition to your family potluck or Sunday dinner. It is also a meal in a jar recipe. You can keep it long-term! How cool is that? Unlike the other jar recipes, it uses some mayonnaise or olive oil in the preparation. If you add it to your longer-term storage, be sure you have the oil or mayonnaise stored as well so you will be able to prepare it.

CLASSIC PEA SALAD

TESS-A-RONI

1 cup long grain rice

½ cup fideo noodles (or angel-hair pasta, broken small)

Seasoning (in a snack-size baggie separate from the rice and noodles but in the same resealable bag or pint jar):

1 Tbsp. bouillon (low sodium, no MSG)

2 tsp. Chef Tess All Purpose seasoning mix

At service you need:

2 Tbsp. butter or oil

2 cups water (or broth if you didn't use bouillon)

1 cup cubed chicken, pork, or beef (optional)

Directions: In a 1-quart covered pan, brown the rice and noodles in the oil until noodles are a nice, deep brown but not burned. Add water and contents of the seasoning bag. Bring to a boil and then cover and reduce heat to low for 20–25 minutes.

For storage, I keep the rice and noodles in sandwich-size sealable bags or in a pint jar with an oxygen absorber.

Different-flavored Tess-a-Roni mixes:

Mexican rice: Use 1 tablespoon dehydrated onion and 1 tablespoon carrot, but for seasoning use 1½ tsp. Chef Tess Southwest Fajita seasoning instead of All Purpose.

Oriental Flavor: Use 1 tablespoon onion, 1 tablespoon carrot, and celery seed, but also add ¼ cup soy sauce in place of the bouillon and 1 teaspoon curry or Chinese five spice. At preparation time, use 1 teaspoon sesame oil with the regular oil.

Note: You can add hydrated freeze-dried vegetables to your Tess-a-Roni when you add the water. It adds a lot of depth to the side dish. My favorite is adding hydrated Honeyville freeze-dried peas.

SOUTHWEST SWEET POTATO GRATIN

SOUTHWEST SWEET POTATO GRATIN

3 cups Honeyville freeze-dried sweet potatoes, hydrated according to package directions

¾ cup Honeyville freeze-dried cheddar cheese, hydrated with a mist of cold water

Cheese sauce:

2 Tbsp. Honeyville dehydrated butter

1 tsp. chicken bouillon (no MSG, low sodium)

¼ cup Honeyville dehydrated green onion

⅓ cup Honeyville cheese sauce powder

1 Tbsp. Chef Tess Southwest Fajita seasoning

1 tsp. ancho chile powder

¾ cup Honeyville sour cream powder

⅛ tsp. pepper

1½ cups water

Directions: In a medium pot, combine sauce ingredients and whisk well over low heat 4–5 minutes until smooth. In a lightly oiled casserole dish, place half of the hydrated sweet potato. Cover with half of the sauce and half of the cheese. Repeat layers. Cover with foil and bake in your solar oven or regular oven at 325 degrees, 25–30 minutes. Remove from the oven and allow to sit for 5 minutes before serving.

I developed this recipe when I was tired of the same old sweet potato casserole for Thanksgiving. A star was born. It's savory and carries a little heat. I think it's just evil . . . and good.

HOMEMADE STOVE-COOK STUFFING

6 cups cubed bread (make sure the pieces are pretty small)

1 Tbsp. dry parsley flakes

1 Tbsp. chicken bouillon (I like the no MSG or low sodium variety)

¼ cup Honeyville freeze-dried onion

½ cup Honeyville freeze-dried celery

1 Tbsp. Chef Tess All Purpose seasoning mix

2 tsp. garlic powder

2 tsp. ground pepper

Directions: Preheat oven to 350 degrees. Bake bread 8–10 minutes on a sheet pan—it may take longer depending on the size of the cubes of bread (it should be dry!). In large bowl, toss bread with remaining ingredients until evenly coated. Store in an airtight container. This will keep for 1–4 months or 12 months if frozen.

To prepare: For 4 (½-cup servings), combine 2 cups stuffing mix with ½ cup water and 2 tablespoons melted butter. To make a full batch, for 7 cups stuffing total, combine 1½ cups water and ⅓ cup butter. Microwave 3–5 minutes or, on the stovetop, boil water and butter, and add stuffing mix. Simmer on low 3–5 minutes. Cover and allow to steam 5 minutes more. Serve hot.

Use Homemade Stove-Cook Stuffing instead of potatoes and control the sodium content, flavors, and ingredients! Plus, you can make this using gluten-free bread in place of the regular bread, and suddenly you have a complete, less expensive alternative to store-purchased mixes!

HOMEMADE STOVE-COOK STUFFING

HOMEMADE NOODLES

2 cups Honeyville semolina flour or Honeyville organic Kamut® flour

1/3 cup Honeyville whole egg powder

½ tsp. salt or Chef Tess All Purpose seasoning mix

½ tsp. onion powder or ¼ tsp. garlic

¾ cup water

Directions: Combine dry ingredients. Add water to the mix (or ½ cup water and ¼ cup puree of spinach or tomato if you want a veggie noodle) and knead until it's a smooth dough. Make it into noodles.

Knead the dough a few minutes until it gets well combined and a lot smoother. It will still look a little rough, but the whole wheat is that way. Divide into 2 balls. Take one of the balls of dough and roll it out on a well-floured tabletop, about ½ inch thick and 2 feet long.

Fold dough into thirds like a travel brochure. Roll out the dough again on a well-floured surface until it is about 3 feet long. Repeat the folding step and roll one last time until it is very thin, about ⅛ inch or less. Mine is so thin you can almost see through it. A well-floured tabletop will really help this process, but also some good muscles applying the pressure to the center of the rolling pin instead of the handles. When rolled out, it is about 5 feet long.

With a sharp knife or pizza cutter, make the cuts for the noodles. Make sure you get through all of the dough and the noodles are about ¼ inch wide and 12 inches long. Repeat the whole process with your second ball

Have you ever wanted to make your own pasta? Did you know you can do it using completely dry ingredients from food storage?

of dough. Transfer the noodles to a drying rack and allow to air-dry a few minutes. This is when I start my water boiling to cook the noodles. If you want them to air-dry a few hours, that works as well.

Bring a gallon of water to a rolling boil. Add plenty of salt to the water. Put the noodles in all at once and cook 2–4 minutes (depending on how long you let them dry). Drain and lightly drizzle with olive oil. Top with sauce or serve with cooked sausage, olives, tomatoes, cheese . . . whatever you love.

HOMEMADE BUTTERMILK RANCH DRESSING

1 cup low-fat mayonnaise

¼ cup Honeyville buttermilk powder plus 1 cup water

2 tsp. onion powder

½ tsp. garlic granules

2 Tbsp. fresh chopped parsley (or 1 Tbsp. dry)

salt and fresh cracked pepper

dash of dill or paprika (if desired)

Directions: Mix all ingredients together with a whisk until smooth.

Homemade salad dressing not only saves money, it also tastes amazing! Here are a few of my favorite recipes.

FRENCH DRESSING

Mix:

- 1 tsp. dry mustard
- 1 tsp. paprika
- 1 tsp. Real Salt
- ½ tsp. pepper
- 1 Tbsp. Honeyville lemonade powder
- 1 Tbsp. sugar
- 1 Tbsp. Honeyville freeze-dried onion
- 1 tsp. garlic powder

Directions: Combine dry ingredients. In a pint-size Mason jar, combine ¾ cup vegetable oil, ¼ cup apple cider vinegar, and the dry ingredients. Tightly secure lid. Shake bottle a minute or two until dressing is well combined. Put in fridge overnight for flavors to marry completely. Use anywhere you would use French dressing.

French Dressing is one of the most classic flavors for dressing, and when it's made from scratch, it's one of my favorites! Here's my variation using the light lemon flavor of the Honeyville lemonade mix as well as the remarkably fresh taste of freeze-dried onions.

BASIC PASTA SALAD

BASIC PASTA SALAD

1 lb. pasta of your choice, cooked al dente and seasoned well with salt and pepper

1 cup chopped bell pepper (¾ cup freeze-dried bell pepper, hydrated, will work)

1 cup carrots, shredded or chopped (¾ cup dehydrated carrot, hydrated, will work)

1 stalk celery, sliced thin (½ cup freeze-dried celery, hydrated, will work)

½ medium red onion, sliced thin or chopped fine (½ cup freeze-dried onion, hydrated, will work)

Basic Vinaigrette:

¾ cup olive or vegetable oil (flavored oils are great)

¼ cup red wine vinegar or cider vinegar

1 tsp. fresh pressed garlic

herbs and spices

salt

pepper

Herbs are the aromatic leaves, flowers, and stems of plants. Fresh or dry herbs work. Make sure you smell the jar. If it smells like the spice or herb, then the stuff inside is still full of flavor. Spices are seeds and bark. They will need to be ground or grated. If you don't have a spice mill (not many do), just buy them preground and be sure they're fresh.

How many of you just read "herb and spices" and panic hit? I hear you saying, "I don't cook like that . . . I need a recipe." Am I right? This is where I want you to try to let go of your cooking inhibitions and think with your heart. My twelve-year-old does it; you definitely can do it! I believe in you. For one batch of salad, you will need one batch of salad dressing.

I want to help you listen to the culinary artist in yourself as well as teach you the basics of cooking. That means I will give a basic recipe and then some wonderful ideas of flavors that would go with it. I will be listing some basic spices and herbs that work together. The lists are not complete. (This would take pages and pages. Remember that this is the beginning—the basics.) I have used this recipe in cooking classes for several years. It works. I use it all the time in my home as well. It's vastly inexpensive and saves you real money.

DRESSING VARIATIONS

The following are herb and spice flavors that work together. It is not a complete list, but it is a good start.

Italian:

HERBS: basil, rosemary, thyme, flat leaf parsley, marjoram
SPICES: fennel, caraway, crushed red pepper, celery seed
FLAVOR AGENTS: hard cheeses like Parmesan and Asiago, olives, roasted peppers, citrus zest, capers

Greek:

HERBS: dill, oregano, rosemary, mint, parsley
SPICES: fennel, anise, black pepper, dill seed
FLAVOR AGENTS: feta cheese, olives, pickled peppers

Asian:

HERBS: cilantro, mint, lemon grass, sesame oil (use 2 tsp. in place of some of the oil)
SPICES: cumin, chile paste, curry paste, fennel, ginger
FLAVOR AGENTS: lime zest, soy sauce, hoisin sauce, citrus zest, peanuts, cashews

Mexican:

HERBS: cilantro, oregano, thyme
SPICES: cumin, coriander, chile pods, black pepper, allspice
FLAVOR AGENTS: lime zest, roasted corn, green onions, radish, and black olives

Toss the herbs and spices in the Basic Vinaigrette. If you are unsure about the impact a spice or herb will have on your dressing, I suggest you start with ½ teaspoon of seasonings and taste the dressing as you continue to add different flavors. You will then begin to understand the impact each new spice will have on dressings in the future. It's a learning process. Start with a small amount and work up to more as your confidence increases. The flavor agents can be added directly to the basic pasta salad recipe. Mix and match fresh veggies as they are in season. Add fruit if you like.

For hearty dinners, add some roasted chicken or beef. Marinate meat in the vinaigrette and save a lot of money on those fancy bottles of premade stuff. You can do it. Start to feel yourself free up in the kitchen. It is liberating. Enjoy!

Now for you folks who just want a grab-and-go dressing fix, you can just use the premade spice blends. You know, fajita seasoning, Italian seasoning, Greek seasoning. Don't hurt yourself if you don't feel able to do the artsy stuff yet. I'm patient . . . and it's a process. Feel the love, babe.

Want fat-free salad dressing?

Did you know it's almost free to make if you have cornstarch and juice already in your cupboard? Use ¾ cup vegetable broth or juice and ¼ cup vinegar. In a cold saucepan, combine the vegetable broth with 1 tablespoon cornstarch. Add the liquid slowly and then, when combined, cook on medium heat, boiling until thick, about 5–7 minutes. Allow to cool slightly and then add the vinegar and remaining herbs and spices. Use immediately. Keep refrigerated. If dressing gets thick, simply add a little more vegetable broth to thin it.

WHOLE GRAIN SNACKS

4-GRAIN JAM-FILLED COOKIE MUFFINS

1 cup Honeyville buttermilk pancake mix

2 cups Honeyville 4-grain cereal mix

2 tsp. vanilla

1 tsp. almond extract

½ cup Honeyville granulated honey

⅔ cup water or reconstituted buttermilk powder

Honeyville jam or apple butter of your choice

Directions: Preheat oven to 375 degrees. Combine all ingredients except jam until just mixed. Lightly spray a cookie sheet with nonstick coating. Scoop ⅓ cup cookie batter onto cookie sheet, placed 1 inch apart. With your finger, hallow out a hole in the center, being careful not to go all the way through the dough. Dot a teaspoon or two of jam in the hole. Continue until all the piles of dough have a dot of jam in the middle. Bake 12–15 minutes, until lightly brown.

When I was a little girl, my mother used to make these cookies. Many mornings, I remember smelling spices and oat delight baking in our oven. Nothing says "good morning" better than a wholesome, grab-and-go breakfast! Plus, they are great for snacks. Use the convenience of the Honeyville buttermilk pancake mix as the base, and you'll be surprised how quickly they come together. Be the hero . . . make cookies for breakfast!

4-GRAIN JAM-FILLED COOKIE MUFFINS

GOURMET CHEESE CRACKERS

2½ cups whole wheat pastry flour or 2½ cups all-purpose flour

½ tsp. salt seasoning of your choice (I use Chef Tess All Purpose seasoning mix)

½ tsp. baking powder

1 cup freeze-dried cheddar cheese (or ¾ cup sharp cheddar cheese)

½ cup warm water (¼ cup if fresh cheese used)

¼ cup Lucero olive oil (garlic or lemon are amazing here)

Directions: Preheat oven to 375 degrees. In a bowl, combine the flour, salt seasoning, and baking powder. Combine cheese and water. If you use fresh cheese, use only ¼ cup water. The warmer the water, the better melted the cheese will be, but don't get it too hot or it will be gooey cheese. We want it to be able to blend. If using the freeze-dried cheese, let it soak about 10 minutes. Measure your olive oil. Make sure it's a good oil, folks. I use Lucero olive oil because I adore the flavor. Combine the dry ingredients with the cheese mixture. Add the oil. Mix until just combined. It takes only about a minute. Roll half of dough out on a lightly oiled baking stone. Use a pizza cutter or a pastry cutter to cut the dough into squares. Prick with a fancy cracker-making tool . . . like a fork. I lightly mist the crackers with a little water from a spray bottle and then sprinkle them with seasoning. Bake in preheated oven for 15–20 minutes until crispy. Mmm.

Cheese crackers are a staple in a lot of families. Now you can make them at home and not only completely impress your kids but also save a lot of money in the process.

9-GRAIN GOURMET ONION CHEESE CRACKERS

- ½ cup Honeyville cheese sauce powder
- ½ cup Honeyville sour cream powder
- 2 cups Honeyville 9 grain flour
- ½ tsp. baking powder
- ½ tsp. salt
- 1 tsp. onion powder
- ½ tsp. garlic powder
- ¼ cup olive oil
- ¾ cup water

Directions: Preheat oven to 375 degrees. In a bowl, combine the cheese sauce powder, sour cream powder, 9 grain flour, baking powder, salt, onion powder, and garlic powder. In a separate bowl, combine the oil and water. Pour oil and water over the dry ingredients and knead lightly 2–3 minutes. Divide dough into two balls. Roll half of dough out on a well-oiled baking stone until a uniform ¼ inch thick. Use a pizza cutter or a pastry cutter to cut the dough into squares. Prick with a fancy cracker-making tool . . . like a fork. Lightly mist crackers with a little water from a spray bottle and then sprinkle with salt or Chef Tess All Purpose seasoning. Bake in preheated oven for 15–20 minutes until crispy.

Do you love crackers but wonder if you can save money or make them more nutritiously at home? Homemade crackers are crisp, delicious, and amazing. They saved our family budget immensely when the children were small, and now I can't live without homemade crackers around. Be sure to oil your baking sheets well and to use a light hand when rolling out this delicate dough. The beauty of the Honeyville 9 grain flour will shine through, giving these a lightly nutty flavor. The complementing flavors of the cheese, sour cream, and onion will really impress.

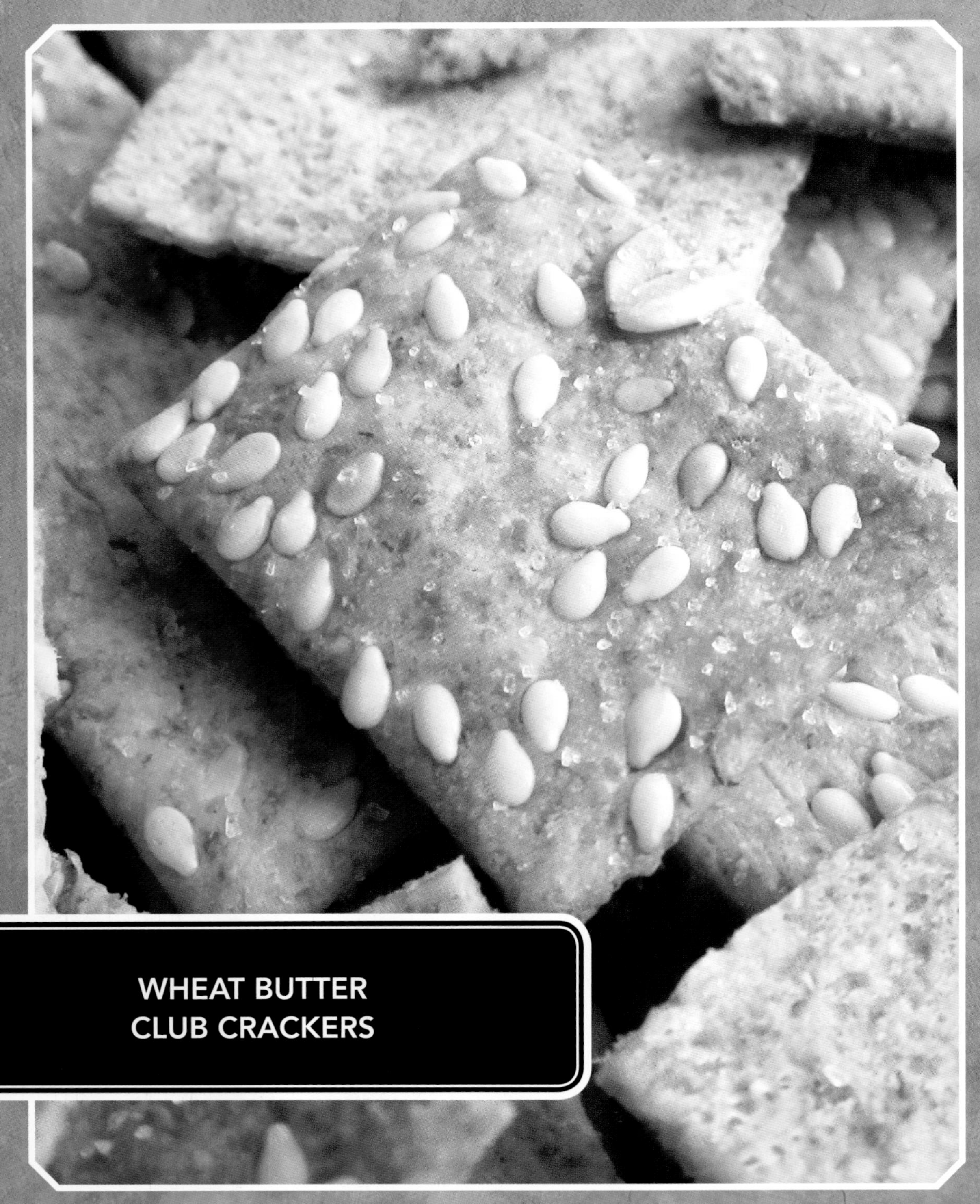

WHEAT BUTTER CLUB CRACKERS

WHEAT BUTTER CLUB CRACKERS

3 cups whole wheat pastry flour

½ cup white corn flour

1 cup Honeyville powdered butter (or 1¼ cups real butter, softened)

1 tsp. salt

1 tsp. baking powder

1¼ cups water

Directions: Combine the dry ingredients well in a medium-sized bowl. If you use real butter, work it into the dry ingredient mixture as you would for biscuits or pie crust. Preheat oven to 375 degrees. Roll half of dough out on a lightly oiled baking stone.

Use a pizza cutter or pastry cutter to cut the dough into squares. Prick with a fancy cracker-making tool . . . like a fork. I lightly mist the crackers with a little water from a spray bottle and then sprinkle with seasoning. Bake for 15–20 minutes until crispy.

I love club crackers. Who doesn't? They are beautifully crispy and light. I love this whole wheat version for how light and flaky it is. You can also mix a few tablespoons of Honeyville 6 grain rolled cereal into the dough before rolling it. I love how those whole grains make the crackers taste and add some hearty flavor. Another favorite thing to do is sprinkle the dough with a light mist of water and then top with whole brown flaxseed. Lightly roll them into the dough with a rolling pin and then cut the dough as you would for the crackers. White sesame seeds are also perfect for these little crisp wafers, along with some natural sea salt.

SOFT, SWEET-N-SALTY WHOLE GRAIN-N-SEED PRETZELS

2 cups warm water (no hotter than 110 degrees)

1 Tbsp. sugar

¼ cup olive oil

1 Tbsp. active dry yeast (1 pkg.)

4½ cups Honeyville Mountain Mills whole wheat flour

¼ cup Honeyville teff

2 Tbsp. Honeyville sesame seeds

2 Tbsp. Honeyville flaxseeds

2 tsp. salt

Prep equipment:

parchment paper

vegetable oil

10 cups water

⅓ cup baking soda

1 large egg yolk

1 tsp. water

pretzel salt or kosher salt

crystal cake decorating sugar (Any color! Be creative.)

Directions: Combine the water, sugar, oil, and yeast in a small bowl. In a 1-gallon bowl, combine the flour, teff, seeds, and salt. Knead 5 minutes by hand or 4 minutes by machine. Form dough into a ball and place in a gallon-size bucket or bowl with a lid. Allow to rise 1 hour (until your finger inserted in the dough leaves a hole.)

Preheat oven to 450 degrees. Line 2 sheet pans with parchment paper and lightly brush with vegetable oil. Set aside. Bring 10 cups of water with the baking soda to a rolling boil in an 8-quart, 14-inch deep skillet. Divide the dough into 8 portions for large pretzels. Fold each into a rectangle. Roll tightly using your magical, skilled, nimble fingers and pinch as you go. Roll into a 24-inch strand of dough. Place the pretzels on a parchment-lined

cookie sheet. Raise 15 minutes. Gently lift up pretzels and place in boiling water for 30 seconds or so. Really, that's not too long. It's just long enough. I use a large, slotted spatula to remove them from the water and let them drain well. Place the moistened pretzels back on the cookie sheets, 4 to a sheet. Combine the egg yolk with a teaspoon of water and whisk well.

With a pastry brush, carefully paint the tops of the pretzels with the egg yolk mixture. Then . . . we sprinkle ours with some colored sugar and kosher sea salt. Don't feel like you have to use the colored stuff . . . I just think it looks really fun!

Transfer trays to your 450-degree oven and bake 15–17 minutes.

ROLLS, SWEET ROLLS & FREEZER BREADS

5-DAY SWEET ROLL DOUGH

⅔ cup Honeyville instant powdered milk (or 4 cups prepared homemade soy milk)

1 cup Honeyville vanilla instant pudding mix (or homemade instant pudding mix)

½ cup Honeyville whole egg powder

¾ cup Honeyville butter powder

¾ cup sugar

¾ cup olive oil

6 cups water (at 110 degrees or less)

2 Tbsp. active dry yeast

1 Tbsp. baking powder

12–13 cups bread flour

1 Tbsp. salt

Directions: Combine the powdered milk, vanilla pudding mix, egg powder, butter powder, sugar, and oil in a 3-gallon food-grade bucket. Add the water one cup at a time with a whisk until all water is added and smooth mixture is made. Add the yeast and baking powder along with 4 cups of flour. Mix with a wooden spoon until smooth batter forms. Add the salt and 5–6 more cups flour, kneading well after each addition of flour. Mix 5 minutes. Allow dough to rest 10 minutes. Add 2–3 more cups flour, depending on how moist the dough is. Knead 3 minutes more (total kneading time: 5–6 minutes on medium speed with a dough hook or 600 turns by hand). Form into a nice ball and put in an ungreased food-grade bucket in your fridge overnight (at least 8 hours). Punch down. This dough is good up to 7 days in the fridge.

To bake, remove dough from fridge. Form into 2-oz. rolls. Place 1 inch apart on greased pan and allow to rise 1–1½ hours at room temperature.

Yields 6 dozen medium rolls.

…is dough is good …your fridge up to …days. I call it 5-day …ugh, but it will last …nger. The beauty …this dough is that …u can make rolls or …eet rolls every day …the week, or just …ke it enough ahead …time that it's good … a big event like …anksgiving.

5-DAY SWEET ROLL DOUGH

FREEZER-TO-OVEN READY ROLL DOUGH

Combine:

- 1½ cups water (no hotter than 110 degrees)
- 2 tsp. active dry yeast
- 3 Tbsp. Honeyville granulated honey
- 4¼ cups Honeyville all purpose flour (whole wheat works too)
- 2 tsp. salt
- 6 Tbsp. oil
- 3 Tbsp. Honeyville whole egg powder

Directions: Combine everything in one large bowl or mixer. Knead 5 minutes by hand or 3 minutes in a mixer on medium setting. This is a less-developed dough as far as gluten is concerned. Form into a ball and place in a bowl covered with plastic or a lid for 1 hour, or until doubled in size. Punch down dough and divide into 2 pieces. I put them in a log form, which helps to keep the size of the dough balls pretty even. You can get science-like and weigh the dough and then divide it into 24 equal portions. Divide the two logs in half again, so you have 4 logs. Each one will get cut into 6 pieces. See . . . you will have to use a little math, but I think you can handle it. I really do.

Now, lightly (I do mean lightly) dust the countertop with a little flour—just a little. We don't want the rolls sticking too much. On the other hand, we don't want so much flour that they just roll all over the place. The point is, we want a little tacky stuff so they form correctly. Take the dough piece and pinch the sides together. Then turn it over so the pinched side is down. I keep a combination of what I call "everything bagel topping." It's basically ¼ cup sesame seed, ¼ cup poppy seeds, 2 tablespoons kosher salt, 2 tablespoons dry onions, and 1 tablespoon dehydrated minced garlic. If desired,

This recipe yields 24 rolls and can easily be doubled. The convenience of these rolls cannot be beat. There's no need to wait for the rolls to rise out of the freezer. They are ready to bake!

roll each roll in this mixture and place 1 inch apart on a greased pan that will fit in your freezer.

Allow to rise at room temperature, uncovered, for 35–40 minutes, until the rolls are touching if originally placed 1 inch apart. Cover with foil and place in the freezer. Keep frozen up to 1 month.

Removing them from the pan once frozen and placing them directly in a freezer bag will save space in your freezer . . . big time!

To Bake: When you want fresh rolls, preheat oven to 375 degrees. Remove rolls from the freezer. (Important note: Don't place glass pans directly from the freezer to the oven; they will shatter.) If you keep rolls frozen in freezer bags, place frozen rolls on a greased pan and then place in the oven. Bake 20–25 minutes until golden brown. Try not to eat them all in one sitting.

COTTAGE CHEESE DILL ROLLS

1 tsp. dry yeast

½ cup warm water (under 110 degrees)

2 Tbsp. sugar

¾ cup small-curd cottage cheese (homemade or reconstituted freeze-dried)

2 Tbsp. Honeyville whole egg powder

2 Tbsp. Honeyville dehydrated green onion

1½ tsp. dry dill

½ tsp. baking soda

2 cups all-purpose flour

Egg wash:

2 Tbsp. Honeyville whole egg powder

¼ cup water, whisked well

real kosher salt

Directions: Preheat oven to 350 degrees. Proof the yeast, water, and sugar in a small bowl for 5 minutes. In a large bowl, mix together the cottage cheese, egg powder, onion, dill, and baking soda.

Add the yeast and mix. Add the flour and knead until you have a firm but smooth dough. Let double in size. Form into 2-ounce balls and let rise again until doubled in size. Mix the egg and water together to make an egg wash. Paint the rolls with the wash and garnish with a good amount of kosher salt. Bake in oven until golden brown. (It took 20 minutes in my oven, and I rotated them halfway through.)

This recipe yields 10–12 rolls. I bake mine on stoneware. If you want to make this into a gorgeous loaf, double the recipe ingredients. Knead and

raise according to directions but form into a loaf and place into a greased 8-inch loaf pan. Raise until doubled. Paint the loaf with egg wash. Preheat oven to 425 degrees. Bake at 425 degrees for 15 minutes and then lower to 350 for 15–20 more minutes or until internal loaf temperature is over 175 degrees.

Note to my whole grain bakers: Whole wheat flour can be used. I prefer white wheat, a whole grain flour or fresh, home-ground flour from hard white wheat. Do not use soft wheat because this will not give enough protein for good bread.

OAT ROLLS

3 cups rolled oats

2½ cups water or milk (no hotter than 110 degrees)

½ cup honey

¼ cup olive oil

2 tsp. yeast

3 cups Honeyville UltraGrain white wheat bread flour

1 Tbsp. salt

Directions: Combine first five ingredients. Allow oats to absorb the water and the yeast to get hyperactive. This usually takes about 30 minutes. On the plus side, this softens the oats without cooking the starch. It is important to not use cooked oats, because the gummy cooked oats will lead to an undesirable roll. Starch will still cook but not be gummy. You will have a nice tender roll.

Add flour and salt. You may need more or less flour depending on the storage conditions of the flour. I usually opt for less flour whenever possible. It makes pretty stiff dough. I knead by hand in the bowl and avoid using too much flour. Do 300 turns or use a mixer for 3–4 minutes on medium speed. Form into a ball and allow to rise until doubled.

Allow the dough to rise and then use the roll-molding techniques (used in Freezer-to-Oven Ready Roll Dough directions on page 122).

Yields 24 rolls.

In the case of this dough, I have found steaming the rolls in a covered, clay crock to be by far my favorite baking method. I also use this dough to make a loaf of bread. This is done when a sheet pan is lightly oiled and then a free-standing large, double loaf using all the dough is made. For rolls, allow rolls to rise until twice their size and very fluffy. Bake in oven preheated to 425 degrees 30–35 minutes (or until internal temperature reaches 170 degrees). Allow to cool before slicing.

You will find these rolls to be very moist and have a shelf life of 3–4 days, if they're not eaten before then.

To make this bread an Italian sourdough: Use 1 cup sourdough starter in place of 1 cup of the water and add ¼ cup more water if necessary. I also use basil-infused oil in place of the oil and 1 tablespoon minced garlic, 1 tablespoon minced fresh rosemary, and ¼ cup minced fresh Italian parsley. Mix all the herbs into the dough in the beginning.

AUNTIE EM'S ONION SANDWICH ROLLS

- ¾ cup lukewarm milk
- 5 Tbsp. lukewarm water
- 3 Tbsp. butter, softened
- 1½ Tbsp. salt
- 3 Tbsp. white sugar
- 1 tsp. onion powder
- 3 Tbsp. Honeyville freeze-dried onion
- ¼ cup Honeyville instant potato flakes
- 3 cups all-purpose flour
- 1 Tbsp. active dry yeast
- 1 egg white
- 1 Tbsp. water
- ¼ cup dried minced onion

Directions: Place lukewarm milk and water, butter, salt, sugar, onion powder, freeze-dried onion, potato flakes, flour, and yeast into the pan of a bread machine in the order recommended by manufacturer. Select the dough cycle and press "start." When the cycle has completed, remove the dough from the machine and knead on a lightly floured surface. Cut into 8 equal pieces and form into balls. Gently flatten the balls until they are 4 inches in diameter. Place in a draft-free place to rise until double in size, about 40 minutes. Preheat the oven to 350 degrees. Whisk the egg white and water in a cup. Brush over the tops of the risen rolls and sprinkle with minced onion. Bake for 15–20 minutes, until golden brown.

I especially love how light and fluffy they are! Well done! Thanks, Auntie Em, for a great recipe!

My sister, Emily, shared this sandwich roll recipe with me. No matter what I serve them with, they are eaten with love. Em uses the convenience of her bread machine's dough setting to make these rolls. I mix them by hand and get great results as well.

AUNTI EM'S ONION SANDWICH ROLLS

PUMPKIN AND SPICED PEACH STICKY BUNS

- 1 cup warm milk (under 110 degrees)
- 2 tsp. active dry yeast (1 pkg.)
- 1/3 cup sugar
- 1 cup packed canned pumpkin
- 1 tsp. salt
- ¼ cup oil
- 4 cups flour
- 1 tsp. cinnamon
- ½ tsp. nutmeg
- ½ tsp. almond extract

- ¾ cup sugar-free peach spread
- 2 Tbsp. Chef Tess Wise Woman of the East spice blend

Topping:

- ¾ cup light brown sugar
- ¼ cup unsalted butter
- ¼ cup honey (caramel honey sauce is amazing here)
- 1½ cups (6 oz.) coarsely chopped pecans

Directions: Put the milk, yeast, sugar, and pumpkin in a mixer with a whisk and mix until smooth. Add remaining ingredients from first section. Mix with a dough hook until smooth and elastic, about 5 minutes (by hand about 300 turns). Put dough in a covered bowl and raise about 1 hour until doubled. Lightly flour a countertop and roll dough to ½-inch thickness, a rectangle of 12 inches by 18 inches. Spread peach spread over dough and sprinkle with spice blend. Roll tightly and pinch seam. Cut into 2-inch wedges. Make the topping: in a 1-quart saucepan, combine brown

sugar, butter, and honey over low heat; stir until sugar and butter are melted. Pour mixture into a greased 9 × 13 pan and sprinkle pecans on top. Place one inch apart. Allow to raise until doubled in size, about 1 hour and 30 minutes. Preheat oven to 375 degrees. Bake buns until golden, 30 to 35 minutes. Remove pan from oven and immediately invert onto a serving tray or baking dish. Let buns cool slightly and serve warm.

WHOLE GRAIN BREADS

BOLD BETTER BREAD WORKSHOP

If you have not been able to attend one of my bread classes, then this chapter is for you. I will be covering what I normally cover with my students. I think it is most helpful when you are beginning to understand some bread basics.

I am the daughter of a woman who believes in great bread. It is in my roots, and making great bread was a skill she taught me from the time I was small. Her first degree is in Home Economics Education, and she was, and is always, great at teaching the science behind bread and its composition. It came in quite handy during my pastry classes in culinary school. It also has come in handy for me working in the pastry shop at the Phoenician resort, running a bakery, and running my own home kitchen. Understanding the basics of wheat flour can change the way you not only make bread but also cakes, cookies, and pastries, as well as thickening puddings and sauces. I will be focusing on wheat flour specifically. I hope that my experience will help others in developing their own skills in this wonderful area that is quickly becoming a lost art. I will be covering six general areas in this workshop: the qualities of good bread, necessary equipment, ingredients, temperatures, dough-handling skills, and the fermentation process. First, a couple notes:

Keeping Quality

Good bread stays fresh for a reasonable length of time and does not dry out or get stale quickly. Do not store in the refrigerator—this will actually hasten the staling process.

Standard-Sized Loaf Pan

This size pan (8 × 4) will permit a well-shaped loaf. It makes a slice of bread, which has the same dimensions both directions, just the right size for the toaster. The baking time given with these recipes is based on a standard-sized loaf pan. If the standard amount of dough goes in a larger pan, it makes a poorly shaped loaf, which is fat and squatty with no oven spring. If you use a larger pan and put more dough in it, you will still have a poorly shaped loaf. The larger pan is too wide to permit an evenly rounded dome on the top of the loaf. The spread is too great, and the dough collapses in the middle.

GENERAL APPEARANCE OF GOOD BREAD

SHAPE: Good bread is symmetrical in shape with good volume. It is smooth on top with no bulges or lumps. It has a well-rounded dome showing good "oven spring". It has an even, "shredded" break around the sides of the loaf, just above the top edge of the pan.

OVEN SPRING: This is the quick rising that takes place during the first ten minutes after bread goes into a hot oven. Oven spring happens before the heat sets the cell walls and before the bread starts to brown.

COLOR: The color of good bread is rich golden-brown on all sides. The top of the loaf may be slightly darker brown than the sides or bottom.

SLICE SIZE: Slices cut from the center of a well-shaped loaf are only slightly larger than those cut near the ends. A good loaf gives a slice of bread which measures about the same both directions.

CRUST: On high-quality bread, the crust is thin, crisp, and tender.

CRUMB: Color of wheat bread is uniformly cream tan. Texture shows moderately small, rather uniform cells with thin cell walls. Good bread is free from streaks of flour or extremely close grain. The freshly cut surface has a velvety feel, both to your fingers and to your tongue. As you press the crumb, it is soft, elastic, and springy. There are no hard spots or knots in the crumb of high-quality bread.

FLAVOR: The flavor of good bread is rather mild. It has the sweet nut-like flavor of the wheat. Good bread has good eating quality, even when it isn't still warm! Both the flavor and texture combine to create excellence in bread. It is not yeasty, salty, or sour (except in the case of sourdough).

Breadmaking Equipment:

- measuring cups
- measuring spoons
- spatula or straightedge knife for leveling
- pans or bowl to mix and store all ingredients
- digital or meat thermometer
- large bowl for mixing
- mixer; if you use one. I mix by hand in a food-grade plastic bucket, and it works wonderfully!
- straight-sided crock (to hold fermenting dough)*
- wooden spoon or rubber scraper
- pastry brushes
- plastic wraps, to cover dough during rising to prevent drying
- sharp knives, for cutting dough at molding time
- cooling rack
- timer

**An earthenware bowl or crock keeps the temperature more consistent than a metal container. It also is easier to judge the volume increase of the dough in a straight-sided container than it is in a round bowl. This can also be said of the bucket method. Food-grade buckets are great for keeping a standard temperature.*

Collect the Right Ingredients:

WHEAT FLOUR: The main ingredient of all my bread in this workshop is wheat flour. I prefer Honeyville Mountain Mills whole wheat flour or UltraGrain white wheat flour for bread; I am also in love with the Honeyville Kamut® flour for its purity and consistency. It's my standard of excellence, in all honesty. If you have a wonderful grain mill, you can make perfect flour from hard white or red wheat for homemade bread. The hard wheat makes the best bread. Period.

LIQUID: Flour dries out quickly in dry climates. If you live in a dry climate, use more liquid in proportion to flour—this keeps the dough soft enough to make good bread.

MILK: Bread made with milk has more food value. Honeyville makes a baker's dry milk that is made specifically for bread baking. I adore it!

SHORTENING: Shortening is basically any fat. This contributes to a tender loaf and conditions the gluten. The leaner the dough, the higher chance the bread will dry out.

SALT: Salt is not just for flavor; it actually regulates fermentation of the yeast and enhances the gluten structure.

YEAST: What is yeast? Essentially it's a living organism that "eats" simple sugars and expels gas. Make sure your yeast is fresh. It comes in cakes. It's present in sourdough starter. Yes! Yeast is what makes this baby rise!

SUGAR: Natural sugar feeds the yeast and adds to its action.

✳ Watch Your Temperatures:

- Use cool water to soften the yeast. It need not be cold, but it shouldn't be warm enough that you can feel it "warm" on your skin.
- Active dry yeast will die if exposed to temperatures over 110 degrees! Cool the liquid to below 110 degrees before adding the softened yeast.
- Keep to the 85 to 90 degrees rule. I keep fermenting dough at 85 to 90 degrees for uniform rising and best yeast action. It won't taste sour or yeasty. Fermentation is necessary for the gluten to become smooth and more elastic so it can stretch farther and hold more gas.
- Bake bread at 425 degrees. This high temperature at the beginning will stop the yeast action and set the cell walls. Be sure to preheat! Those first fifteen minutes are critical!
- Lower the temperature to 350 degrees after the first 15 minutes—this will prevent the outside from getting too brown before the middle is cooked.

DEVELOP SKILLS IN MOLDING LOAVES

Do not put fat on hands or work surfaces before molding loaves. Fat on hands will leave streaks of fat in the dough, and the dough will not seal properly. This will leave cracks in your finished loaves.

Use very little, if any, flour on work surface. More flour causes heavy streaks of unfermented flour in your finished bread.

Roll out the dough, fold in thirds, and then roll into loaf. This "stacks the structure" of the gluten and makes for a pretty loaf. Fold the other third over the top. Fold it like a brochure . . . well, one made of dough anyway. Now roll and pinch into a log. Place seam-side down in a greased loaf pan. Cover the loaf with a lightly oiled piece of plastic. I prefer to use a bag tented over the pans or to put the loaves in a 12-inch deep, food-safe Rubbermaid or Lexan container with a lid.

- Is it done? A good trick to test the doneness of bread is to use a meat thermometer; the internal temperature should read 170–180 degrees.
- Store bread correctly. Make sure it is kept in a cool place and tightly wrapped. Wait until loaf is cool before wrapping or crust will get soggy.

Correct Dough-Handling Techniques:

- Avoid too much dough.
- Keep dough soft.
- Learn to knead effectively using the push from your shoulders. Practice easy kneading and use palms and heels of the thumb instead of fingers. I personally prefer kneading in a bucket as opposed to using a table. Yes, you can use a mechanical mixer. I prefer having my beginners use their hands; it's almost impossible to over-knead when done by hand, and it helps students to learn to rely on their "baking gut" instead of a machine. That being said, once they've mastered the beginning skills, I think it's perfectly okay to use a mixer, Bosch and KitchenAid being my favorite.
- When kneading is done, form dough into a ball and put into an un-oiled crock. Cover with plastic wrap. Keep dough at 85–90 degrees until ready to punch down.
- Punch dough. Punching is not hitting the dough so much as it is deflating the dough of gas, relaxing the gluten, and equalizing the temperature.

⁂ The Fermentation Process and the Ripe Test:

Do not let dough get too light before first punch down. When cell walls have stretched too far, they will break and affect the texture of the bread.

The dough is "ripe" and ready to be punched down when

- hole made with finger stays in the dough without closing in;
- small creases show on walls of the hole; and
- bubbles or blisters appear near edge of hole.

This is known as fermentation or the process by which yeast acts on the sugars and starches in the dough to produce carbon dioxide and alcohol. An under-fermented dough will not develop proper volume, and texture will be coarse. A dough that ferments too long or at too high a temperature will become sticky, hard to work with, and slightly sour. Again, gluten becomes smoother and more elastic during fermentation, so it can stretch farther and hold more gas. Don't skimp on this process.

There is not any magic chemical, yeast, or mixer that will replace the fermentation process and its ability to change the gluten. *Ever*. Don't be fooled into buying something you don't need. I'm a professional and have rarely used dough enhancers for my bread. Recently I have enjoyed using the Honeyville dough conditioner and vital wheat gluten added to my flour, but they are not necessary for great bread. If you're willing to wait for good bread, it will come to you without the "helpers." Whole grain bread can be made on a budget without a fancy mixer! It's the technique, not the machine, that makes a great baker. In general, I'd much rather see someone starting out with breadmaking buy flour and start mixing by hand and get a feel for bread than ever feel pressured into buying a mixer in order to bake bread. It's a handy tool, but millions of men and women bake remarkable bread without one.

GENEVE'S 5-DAY BREAD

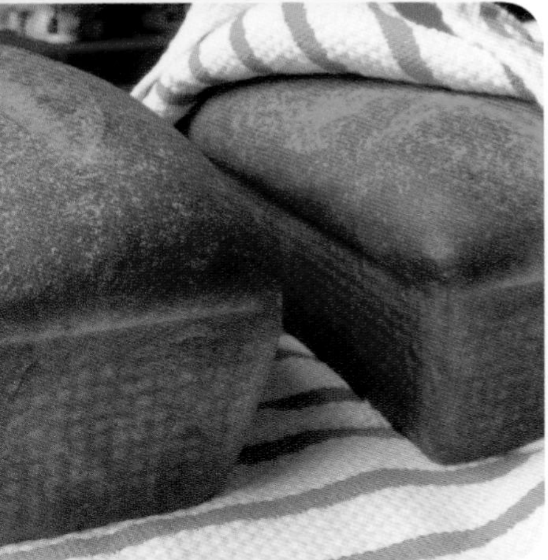

2 Tbsp. active dry yeast (if you are baking at an altitude above 3,000 feet, use 1 Tbsp. only)

4 cups milk (Cold is best. Cold soy milk is wonderful!)

¾ cup honey

4 eggs (or 1 cup egg replacement)

¾ cup oil

1½ cups mashed potatoes, cooled to body temperature again, the consistency of thick oatmeal.

1 Tbsp. baking powder

12–14 cups Honeyville UltraGrain white wheat flour

1 Tbsp. salt

Directions: Dissolve yeast in milk. Stir in honey. Allow yeast to get all foamy and look like it is having a heyday. Add egg, oil, mashed potatoes, baking powder, 4 cups whole wheat flour, and salt, in that order. Do not let yeast come in contact with salt on its own or it will kill the yeast. Beat until smooth. Allow dough to rest 10–15 minutes. Add enough of the flour remaining to make a soft dough that is easy to handle but not dry. Turn dough onto a lightly floured surface and knead for 10 minutes, about 600 turns. If you use an electric mixer with a dough hook, it will take 5–6 minutes on medium speed. Form dough into a ball and place in an ungreased, 2-gallon bowl, covered tightly. If you don't have a large enough bowl, use two smaller bowls. Or half the recipe if you are worried. Put dough in the fridge. Punch down after 2 hours. (This may be faster if you use warm ingredients or flour. If the dough is over 85 degrees when you put it in the fridge, be sure to punch down sooner. Also, if you have kids who open the fridge a lot, be sure to lower the temperature a bit so that your fridge is really as cold as it should be.)

Form into a ball again. Cover tightly and chill for at least 8 hours. Be sure to punch down daily (this not only expels gas but also ensures even temperature in the dough). Shape into 4 loaves. (See loaf molding on pg. 138.

This is my mother's basic sandwich bread recipe that we make on Monday, and then we use the dough throughout the week. It is great to have homemade dough on hand, and it makes for quick breadsticks, pizza crust, rolls, and even bread. Enjoy. This is the recipe that started it all! Thank you, Mom!

I roll the dough out 12 inches by 8 inches, fold into thirds, and roll into a loaf.) Put into well-oiled, 8 × 4 × 4 loaf pans. Larger loaf pans are not recommended.

Cover loaves with a light mist of oil and then cover with plastic for 1½–2½ hours depending on the temperature of your home. Bread will be just over the top of the pan. Make sure oven is preheated to 400 degrees. Bake at 400 degrees for 20 minutes (12–15 minutes above 3,000 feet altitude) and then lower the temperature to 350 degrees and bake an additional 15–20 minutes. (I use a meat thermometer. At 170 degrees the bread is baked through.)

Remove promptly from pans and transfer to a cooling rack. Cool completely before putting in storage bags. Do not store in the fridge.

9-GRAIN CIABATTA WHOLE GRAIN BREAD

Sponge:

- 1 cup Honeyville 9 grain cereal mix (uncooked)
- 1½ cups Honeyville Kamut® flour
- 1¼ cups water (no hotter than 95 degrees)
- 1 Tbsp. active dry yeast

Dough:

- 3 cups water
- 2 Tbsp. olive oil
- 1 Tbsp. salt
- 3 cups Honeyville Kamut® flour

Directions: To make the sponge, combine the sponge ingredients in a 3½-gallon food storage bucket with a lid until it has a batter-like consistency. It will be pretty loose. Cover. After 4 hours remove the lid and check the consistency. When you reach in the bucket, you will find that some strong gluten strands have developed. It's remarkable!

There will also be soft pieces of whole grain in with the gluten development.

To Make The Dough: Add the water to the sponge to break it up. Add the oil, salt, and Kamut® flour. You will not need much more flour than 3 cups. I keep the dough very moist. Again, this helps you to have a nice, tender whole grain bread. Knead by hand for 5 minutes. Fold it over until the rounded part is up. It won't touch the sides of the bucket. After 1½ to 2 hours, it reaches the edges and is quite spongy.

Now, get some Kamut® flour. Spread a generous amount on a countertop or table. Lay out the dough in an 8-inch by 12-inch square, but *do not* expel air. Now, that's totally opposite of any other bread I make, so that might throw you for a loop. Don't be thrown. Just follow what I say and you will be happy. Ahh. Trust is good. Trust Chef Tess . . . (mind control complete.) Top the dough with a good sprinkle of flour. Take out a serrated knife and slice the dough into 4 strips, lengthwise. Lightly oil 2 sheet pans and lay 2 loaves on each pan.

Allow to rise, uncovered, for 1 hour. Preheat your oven to 425 degrees. When the loaf is fluffy enough to pass the edge of the pan, bake it 20–25 minutes. It will get all golden and awe inspiring.

9-GRAIN MOLASSES SANDWICH BREAD

- 2 tsp. active dry yeast
- 3 cups water, 100 degrees
- ½ cup molasses
- ¼ cup olive oil
- 4 cups Honeyville 9 grain flour (plus 1 cup extra for kneading if you need more flour)
- 4 cups Honeyville Mountain Mills whole wheat flour
- 2 tsp. salt
- ½ tsp. baking powder
- ¼ cup Honeyville egg powder
- ¼ cup Honeyville vital wheat gluten powder
- 2 tsp. Honeyville dough conditioner

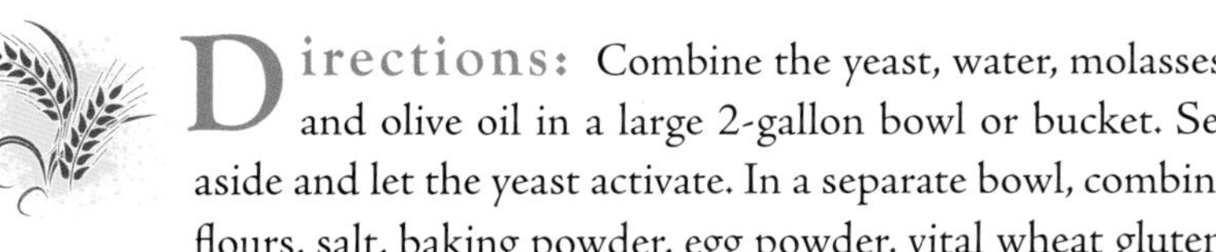

Directions: Combine the yeast, water, molasses, and olive oil in a large 2-gallon bowl or bucket. Set aside and let the yeast activate. In a separate bowl, combine flours, salt, baking powder, egg powder, vital wheat gluten, and dough conditioner. Add the flour mixture to the yeast mixture and stir until well combined. Allow to rest 10 minutes to absorb moisture. This step will help your bread to be moist and tender. Dough will be slightly sticky, but begin to knead (after the ten minute rest) for 5 minutes by mixer (medium speed) or 600 turns by hand until dough is soft and supple. Roll into a ball and place in an un-oiled bowl or covered bucket until doubled in size (about 2 hours in a room around 77 degrees). Punch down the dough and remove from the bowl. Divide into two pieces on a countertop lightly misted with water or a very fine dusting of flour. Do not add much flour to the work surface and do not oil the work surface. Form each piece of dough into a loaf by patting out into a rectangle 8 inches by 18 inches. Fold the rectangle in thirds, like a travel brochure. Roll the dough into a loaf and pinch the ends and seams well. Place seam-side down into an

There's nothing like a soft and smooth slice of slightly nutty whole grain bread nestling tangy cheese, sweet garden tomatoes, and crispy lettuce to make you want to have whole grain every single day! Well, here's a loaf that makes a perfect addition to your lunch, brunch, or dinner. The flavor of the grain is lightly sweetened by the kiss of molasses, and the subtle hint of olive oil will make this a favorite loaf. Because this flour is lower in gluten, you will need to use vital wheat gluten powder.

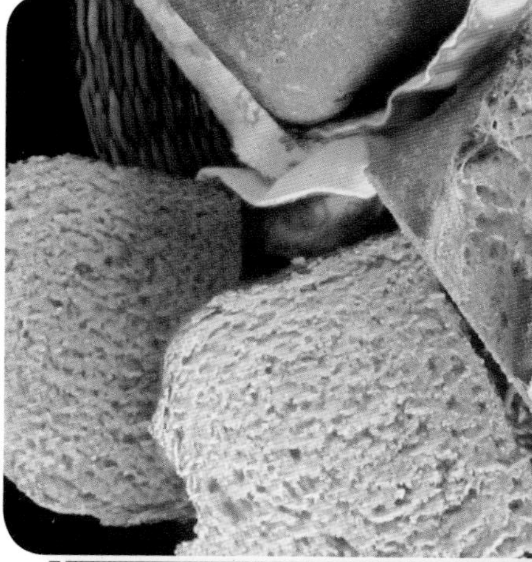

8 × 4, greased loaf pan. Repeat and form your second loaf. Place loaves in a draft-free area, covered loosely with a piece of plastic or a large plastic tub. Allow to rise 1 hour or more, until doubled in size.

Preheat oven to 425 degrees. Place loaves in hot oven and close. Bake 15 minutes at this high temperature. Open oven. Lower temperature to 350 degrees and close oven. Continue baking 20–25 minutes until done (internal temperature of 170 degrees or more). Remove from pans and allow to cool before slicing. Store in a tightly sealed bag to retain moisture.

Yields 2 loaves.

Note: If you use fresh egg, reduce water by ½ cup and use two eggs.

9-GRAIN BANANA-RASPBERRY CHOCOLATE CHIP BREAD

This is one of my favorite whole grain recipes for banana bread because it's perfectly moist and flavorful. The sweetness of the banana is remarkable next to the deep chocolate along with the tartness of the raspberries. The secret is wrapping the loaves of banana bread while they are still slightly warm. The retention of the steam will keep the bread moist and divine.

- 3 cups Honeyville freeze-dried bananas, hydrated in warm water 10 minutes, drained well, and mashed (about 1½ cups mashed bananas)
- 1 cup water
- ¼ cup Honeyville whole egg powder
- 1 tsp. rum flavor extract
- 1 tsp. vanilla
- 1¾ cups Honeyville 9 grain flour
- ¾ cup Honeyville granulated honey
- ¾ cup Honeyville dehydrated butter
- ¼ cup Honeyville banana pudding mix
- ¼ cup Honeyville sour cream powder
- 1 tsp. salt
- 1 tsp. baking soda
- 1 tsp. cinnamon
- ½ cup dark chocolate chips or chocolate chunks
- ½ cup Honeyville freeze-dried raspberries, hydrated 10 minutes and drained well (or ¾ cup frozen berries)

Directions: Preheat oven to 350 degrees. Pour the mashed bananas into a bowl with the 1 cup water, egg powder, rum flavor extract, and vanilla. Stir well. In a separate bowl, measure the flour, granulated honey, dehydrated butter, banana pudding mix, sour cream powder, salt, baking soda, and cinnamon. Combine the dry ingredient mixture with the wet ingredient mixture, just until moistened. Do not overmix. Very gently fold in the chocolate chips and raspberries. Grease a 9 × 5 loaf pan. Coat grease with a thin layer of flour. Put batter in pan and evenly distribute. Then place in the preheated oven for 50–60 minutes, until a toothpick inserted into the loaf comes out fairly clean.

Remove from the pan to a rack. Serve still warm. Wrap tightly with plastic when still slightly warm to preserve the moist texture of the whole grain.

Yields 1 large loaf or 4 mini loaves.

As a child, I used to have thick wedges of corn bread for breakfast drizzled in maple syrup the morning after I'd had corn bread for dinner. The true test of good corn bread is if it will retain it's amazing, tender texture overnight. This passes the test! This is a moist and tender corn bread with 100 percent whole grain goodness in every bite. It's slightly dense and crumbles like authentic Southern corn bread with a lightly sweet taste. Try it with your next hearty chili or as a beautiful breakfast bread with a pat of fresh creamy butter and a drizzle of golden honey.

9-GRAIN SOUTHERN-STYLE SOUR CREAM CORN BREAD

- 2 cups Honeyville corn meal
- 1¾ cups Honeyville 9 grain flour
- 1 tsp. salt
- 2 Tbsp. baking powder
- ½ cup Honeyville granulated honey
- ¼ cup Honeyville whole egg powder
- 1 cup Honeyville sour cream powder
- ½ cup Honeyville butter powder
- 2½ cups water
- ½ cup vegetable oil or melted butter

Directions: Preheat oven to 350 degrees. Combine first 8 ingredients. Add water and ½ cup vegetable oil or melted butter and stir until just combined. Pour batter into a 9 × 13 pan. Bake 30–35 minutes. Test doneness by inserting a skewer or cake tester. If it comes out without batter on it, then the bread is done. If not, put back in the oven for 5–6 minutes. If you're not eating right away, cover corn bread with foil when slightly warm to retain moisture of the whole grain when cooled. Serve warm with baked beans or a little butter and honey. It's also excellent with blueberry sauce, believe it or not.

Note: If you use fresh egg, omit the egg powder. Use 2 eggs and reduce water to 2 cups.

DESSERTS

NUTMEG GINGER APPLE SNAP CRISP

NUTMEG GINGER APPLE SNAP CRISP

Crisp Mix:

- 4 cups Honeyville 4 Grain cereal
- 2 cups brown sugar
- 2 cups Honeyville powdered butter
- 1 Tbsp. Chef Tess Wise Woman of The East spice blend
- 1 tsp. nutmeg (ground)
- 2 tsp. ginger (ground)
- 2 cups toasted sliced almonds or chopped pistachio
- 1 Tbsp. dry lemon zest (or 2 Tbsp. Honeyville lemonade powder)
- 1 Tbsp. salt

Crisp:

- 4 cups Honeyville freeze-dried apples (hydrated with 4 cups hot water 10 minutes and drained well)
- ½ cup Honeyville jam (any flavor)
- ¼ cup water

Directions: Combine all crisp mix ingredients. Divide into 2½-cup portions in wide mouth pint jars or zip-sealing sandwich baggies (yields 4 mixes).

To Make: Combine hydrated apples and jam and place in an 8 × 8 casserole dish. Combine the crisp mix with ¼ cup water. Mix until well crumbly. Spread over the top of the apples mixture. Bake at 350 degrees for 45 minutes until apples are tender. Serve with ice cream if desired.

My kids used to laugh and laugh at the farmer's wife in *Fantastic Mr. Fox* who was famous for her Nutmeg Ginger Apple Snap Cookies. This Apple Crisp is a family favorite that is sure to bring a smile to your face. The dessert mix is so easy to make ahead and have on hand that you'll be happy to share it with those you love.

CRANBERRY CARROT CAKE WITH LEMON CREAM SAUCE

Cake:

- 2 cups Honeyville dehydrated carrots
- 1 cup Honeyville dried cranberries
- 2 cups boiling water
- ½ cup Honeyville powdered whole egg
- 1 cup sugar
- 1 cup Honeyville powdered butter
- 1 tsp. imitation rum extract
- 2 tsp. vanilla bean paste or double strength vanilla
- 1 cup cool water
- 2 cups Honeyville cake flour
- 1 Tbsp. Chef Tess Wise Woman of The East spice blend
- 2 tsp. baking soda
- 1 tsp. Real Salt

Lemon Cream Sauce:

- 3 Tbsp. lemonade powder
- 1 Tbsp. powdered butter
- ¼ cup powdered sour cream
- 3 Tbsp. Ultra Gel
- 1 cup warm water

Directions: Preheat oven to 350 degrees. In a quart-sized bowl, combine carrots, cranberries, and boiling water. Allow to hydrate 20 minutes. Pulse in a food processor a few times to break up the berries and carrots if desired. In a medium-sized separate bowl, combine the powdered egg, sugar, powdered butter, rum extract, and vanilla with the water. Whisk until smooth. Combine the flour, Wise Woman of the East spice blend,

baking soda, and salt in a separate bowl. Add the carrot mixture to the egg mixture and stir well. Add the flour mixture to the carrot-egg mixture and stir by hand 100 turns. Pour into two greased, 9-inch cake pans and bake 30–35 minutes, until a toothpick inserted into the cake comes out clean (a 9 × 13 oblong cake pan takes 40–45 minutes). In a bowl with a 2-cup capacity, combine the lemon cream sauce ingredients. Slowly add warm water while whisking ingredients. Whisk until creamy smooth (about 2 minutes). Pour over slices of cake.

TROPICAL MANGO-BERRY COBBLER

Filling:

2 cups Honeyville freeze-dried mango

1 cup Honeyville freeze-dried strawberries

1 cup Honeyville freeze-dried blackberries

¼ cup Honeyville lemonade mix (any flavor)

½ cup Ultra Gel

1 tsp. almond extract

4 cups water

Tropical Lime Cobbler topping:

2⅓ cups Honeyville buttermilk pancake mix

¼ cup Honeyville powdered butter

1 tsp. dehydrated lime zest

¼ cup Honeyville Tropical Monsoon smoothie mix

⅔ cup coconut milk or prepared strawberry milk

Directions: Combine filling ingredients with 4 cups water. Mix well. Simmer in a saucepan over low heat 10 minutes until fruit is tender and mixture is thick. Allow to cool about 10 minutes more. Combine cobbler topping ingredients. In a medium bowl, combine topping mixture with ⅔ cup coconut milk (or prepared strawberry milk) just until combined. Do not overmix. Preheat your oven to 350 degrees. Put the thickened filling mixture in a 2-quart casserole dish. Drop the cobbler topping mixture on the filling mixture. Bake in oven 45–50 minutes until well cooked. I like to serve it warm, drizzled with Honevyille caramel honey sauce.

TROPICAL MANGO-BERRY COBBLER

FOOD STORAGE PIE CRUST

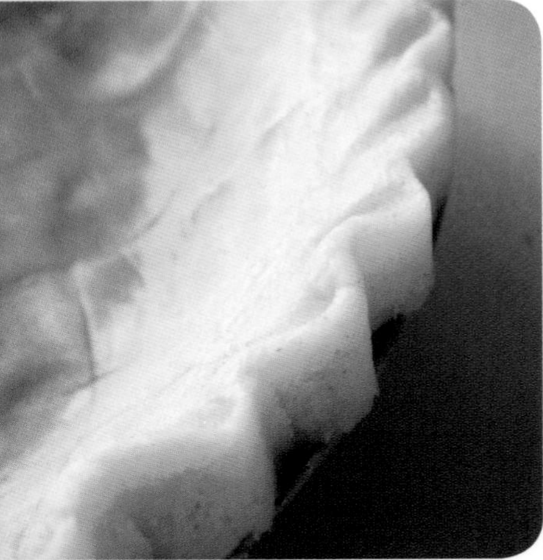

2¼ cups Honeyville pastry flour or all-purpose flour

½ tsp. Real Salt

1 cup Honeyville shortening powder

½ cup Honeyville butter powder

⅓–½ cup + 2 Tbsp. ice-cold water (divided use)

3 Tbsp. white vinegar

Directions: Combine the flour and salt in a bowl. Combine the shortening powder and butter powder very well in a separate large bowl. Add 2 Tbsp. cold water to the dehydrated oils. Make into a paste. Stir well to be sure there are no lumps. Take shortening-butter combination and cut into the flour with a pastry blender. Combine lightly until the mix resembles coarse meal or tiny peas: its texture will not be uniform but will contain small crumbs and small bits and pieces. If you don't have a pastry blender, you can certainly use the wire whisk from your mixer. Or, my personal favorite, the techno-chef fingers. Just make sure your hands are freezing cold. If it's winter, I'm sure you can work that out.

Make a well in the dry stuff and add ⅓ cup cold water and 3 Tbsp. vinegar. I use vinegar in my crust. I have for years. It helps with the flaky texture and it actually does make an amazing crust. Should you doubt me, please, just try it once. If you don't like it, never return to it. I doubt you'll feel that way though. (You may need more or less, so go with 2 Tbsp. of vinegar at first . . . but I can't remember whether the last time I needed to change the recipe and add more water or vinegar than what it says.) Lightly combine the wet and dry ingredients, just until mixed. Overmixing the dough will always result in a hard, non-flake-like crust. You have been warned. Knead it only a few times, making into a ball. Place in a bowl covered with plastic.

Refrigerate about 30 minutes. It will be easier to work with, and it gives the gluten (protein in the wheat) time to rest so the dough will roll out easier.

Forming crust sheets is a simple process: Take half of the dough. With your hands, form it into a patty. I put my dough between two pieces of wax paper. I've used this method since my Granny Barbara W. showed it to me. It's never failed me. Lightly—and I do mean lightly—wipe the countertop with a lightly damp, clean washcloth. Place a piece of wax paper down, about 1 foot by 1 foot. Put the dough down. Top with another piece of wax paper of same proportions. Wax paper helps contribute to a tender crust—using extra flour on the counter instead may lead to a dry crust if overdone. This keeps my crust good and tender. Roll the dough out into a circle. This may take practice to get it just right. Take your time.

Once to the edges of the wax paper, remove the top piece of paper. Place crust, uncovered-side down, in the pan, with an inch or so of crust hanging over the edge of the pan. Now remove the second piece of wax paper. Trim the edge so it hangs over about ¾ inch, then fold it under so it leaves a little rim on the pan. The dough rim comes up about ½ inch. Flute the edges.

To do this, place one finger inside the pan and, with your other hand, pinch on the outside of the dough, pinching the dough between your fingers. You will need a 400 degree preheated oven. I'm not kidding on that point either. It's really important to heat that bad boy up first. Your crust will be better. Now here's what I do: I have these magic regular pinto beans (about ½ cup), see . . . and they go on this layer of aluminum foil, right on top of the crust. They hold the crust down when it bakes so it doesn't get air bubbles. Use dry, uncooked beans . . . not like pork-n-beans from a can. Or, use the fancy pie weights—whatever works. Bake 15–20 minutes, just to make sure it is nice and pre-cooked. Pie dough is good in the fridge up to 4 days.

If you don't plan on baking the pie crust immediately, simply, pat the dough into a ball and wrap tightly with plastic wrap. Allow dough to soften to room temperature a bit before trying to roll it out.

Yields two standard, 9-inch single crust pies using only food storage.

MY FAVORITE PIE CRUST

2¼ cups pastry flour (for whole wheat pastry flour, increase water to about ⅓ cup)

½ tsp. salt

1 cup shortening (Crisco works, but if you want non-trans-fat, try Spectrum brand)

3 Tbsp. cold water

3 Tbsp. vinegar

pie filling of choice

Directions: Mix flour and salt. Cut in shortening with a pastry blender. Combine lightly until the mixture resembles coarse meal or tiny peas: its texture will not be uniform, but will contain small crumbs and small bits and pieces. Sprinkle water and vinegar over mixture one tablespoon at a time and mix lightly with a fork, using only enough water so that the pastry will hold together when pressed gently into a ball. This will vary on the moisture content of the flour.

Divide the dough into two balls. Roll the bottom dough out in a circle 2 inches larger than the 9-inch pie pan (that's 11 inches in diameter); then fit it loosely but firmly into the pan. I do this by lightly folding the dough in half and gently picking it up with my hands. You may roll it out on parchment paper or wax paper to ease this "pick up" process. By far my favorite method is to roll dough between two pieces of parchment paper. I use a light swipe of a damp washcloth first on the counter; this moisture holds the paper in place. Place a piece of wax paper down, about 1 foot by 1 foot. Put the dough down. Top with another piece of wax paper of same proportions. Wax paper helps contribute to a tender crust—using extra flour on the counter instead may lead to a dry crust if overdone. Roll the dough out into a circle. This may take practice to get it just right. Take your time.

Once the dough is rolled, remove the top piece of paper, flip the crust into the pan, and remove the second piece of paper. Roll out the top crust. Fill the pie generously with pie filling of your choice, then put on the top crust and prick in several places with a fork or cut vents. Crimp or flute the edges and bake as directed. I usually cover the edges with a strip of foil or a metal ring called a pie guard. Pie will get nice and brown, but the edges will get almost black without the pie guard.

Yields 2 (9-inch) shells or 1 (9-inch) two-crust pie.

FROZEN PIE TIPS:

- Did you know pie dough is good in the freezer for up to 3 months? Yes! You can make your own freezer pies! Most custard-based pies will become runny, and remember that cornstarch will not hold its thickening once frozen. Ultra Gel will keep its hold. If you thicken your filling with all-natural flour, it will hold forever!
- You can freeze a pie filled with fruit filling and just add 20 minutes to the baking time of the original recipe.
- Freeze uncooked crust in aluminum pie pans, put in a gallon-sized freezer bag, and stack them if you want to maximize freezer space.
- When you want to bake frozen pies, transfer them out of the foil into a stoneware pie plate for crispiest crust.
- Unbaked, frozen pie shells can also be filled with savory fillings like quiche and pot pie stew.
- Now here is the bonus of freezing: Because of the expansion of freezing and defrosting, the protein strands will stretch, break, and become even more tender. Meaning if you freeze your dough, you can count on flakier crust! How cool is that?!

HONEY-FRUITY-CUTIE POPCORN BALLS OF GLORY

- infused extra-virgin olive oil
- ½ cup uncooked Honeyville popcorn
- ½ tsp. Real Salt
- ½ cup granulated sugar
- 1 cup Honeyville honey
- ½ cup Honeyville gelatin (any flavor) or Jello (1 [3-oz.] box, any flavor)

Directions: Over high heat, pour enough oil into the saucepan to cover the bottom of the pan and be about ¼ inch deep. Place three popcorn kernels into the pan and then cover. Once the three kernels have popped, add the remaining kernels. Listen closely to the pan. Once you hear the popping slow substantially, the popcorn is done. Remove from the burner and pour the popped corn into your bowl. Season the popcorn with Real Salt. Combine granulated sugar, honey, and gelatin in a heavy saucepan. Stir slightly and bring to a full rolling boil over medium-high heat. Remove gelatin mixture from stovetop and pour over popcorn. Blend well, until all of the popcorn is coated. Allow to cool a few minutes before shaping into popcorn balls.

Note: You can add up to 1 cup of nuts, candy corns, jelly beans, Boston Baked Beans candy, Red Hots, and so forth at this point.

Shape popcorn into balls using lightly oiled hands, or leave as fruity popcorn, as is. To make a topiary, pierce with a bamboo skewer and tie a ribbon at the base of the ball. You may insert them into other popcorn balls or brownie cupcakes for a standalone topiary or just enjoy a popcorn ball on a stick!

MAGIC FUDGE MIX

- 2 lbs. powdered sugar
- 1 cup Honeyville powdered butter
- 2 cups baker's cocoa
- 1 tsp. salt
- 1 tsp. double-strength vanilla
- ½ tsp. imitation rum extract
- ½ tsp. Chef Tess Wise Woman of The East spice blend
- pinch of cayenne pepper (optional)

Directions: Combine all ingredients until well blended. Place in a gallon-sized freezer bag. I store the bags in the fridge or freezer. Great gift for the holidays! When the holidays get closer, I simply slip the mix into a fabric bag with the mixing directions printed on a cute tag. Give it away not just for the winter holidays but for Mother's Day or any old Tuesday.

To make: Put mix in a microwave-safe bowl with ¾ cup water and heat about 2 minutes. Stir well. Heat one more minute. In the meantime, line an 8 × 8 cake pan with foil and then spray the foil with nonstick coating. Pour the melted mix into the foil-lined pan and top with nuts or dried fruit if desired. Leave pan out to cool 3–4 hours or overnight. Remove fudge from the pan, and remove from the foil. Cut into 1-inch squares.

Yields 4 dozen love bombs, about 4 pounds of fudge.

I developed this fudge mix to give away at the holidays . . . only to find that most of it didn't get given away—we'd eat it before it ever made it out the door! Oh, this is evil . . . but oh so good!

BANANAS FOSTER PEANUT BRITTLE

½ cup salted peanuts

1 cup dehydrated banana chips

½ cup honey

1 cup sugar

½ cup water

1½ Tbsp. butter

1 tsp. baking soda

½ tsp. imitation rum extract

¼ tsp. Chef Tess Wise Woman of the East spice blend (or Saigon cinnamon will work)

Directions: Lightly oil a jelly-roll pan (a cookie sheet with edges so that hot, molten candy doesn't flow all over your kitchen counters). Spread the peanuts and banana chips onto the bottom of the pan. Lightly oil a heat-proof spatula and set it aside. The candy won't stick to it. It's a genius step. Do it. Be a genius and oil the spatula. In a 2-quart kettle or large saucepan, mix together honey, sugar, and water. Stir over medium heat until sugar dissolves. Insert a candy thermometer if using, making certain it does not touch the bottom of the pan (you want to read the syrup temperature, not the pan temperature). Bring mixture to a boil, without stirring. No stirring. I did maybe once, but that was it . . . and it was just at the beginning. *No* stirring after that. Don't do it. You'll get really gritty grainy candy. Early in the cooking process, you can "wash down" any sugar crystals that form on the sides of the pan with a wet pastry brush. I use a silicone brush so I don't get any loose hair in there too.

Remove from heat precisely at 295 degrees (temperature will continue rising) or until drops of syrup form hard, brittle threads in cold water. After boiling action has ceased, add butter. It will steam. Stir a few seconds until it's melted. Now add the baking soda, imitation rum extract, and spice blend. It will bubble up! Stir it to mix in the soda. Don't stir too

Shall we just call this brittle "Bananas Tessalicious"? It's got just the right amount of peanuts, crisp banana chips, and crunchy sweet, lightly spiced candy to almost make you pass out. I'm only saying this so you know that you may need to plan ahead to give it away. (Hint. Hint. I'm almost totally out of brittle.) I for one had to hide it in a closet and lock myself in a different closet, just to avoid the temptation. Evil. Evil. Evil. That's all I can say. Shall I share the recipe then? I think so.

much because you want all that bubble action. When adding flavoring, avoid rising steam. Pour mixture over the bananas and peanuts in the oiled, molten-roll-over-proof pan. Allow to cool 20–25 minutes.

I score it with a sharp knife after about 5 minutes so that it will break in clean cuts. You don't have to do that if you prefer a jagged peanut brittle.

JERRI'S COCONUT BON BONS

almonds (if you want the Almond Joy type)

¾ cup Karo syrup (I use ¾ cup honey)

2½ cups Honeyville macaroon coconut

½–1 tsp. almond extract (depends on how strong an almond flavor you want)

10 oz. chocolate Couverture

Directions: Preheat oven to 400 degrees. Toast the almonds in the oven just until they are warm and you can start to smell them (3–5 minutes); set aside. Bring the Karo syrup or honey to a boil and add the coconut. Remove from heat and add almond extract. Place in fridge until firm. Form into round balls or ovals and place on waxed paper. It helps to moisten your hands a little when making the balls. If desired, press 1 almond to each ball or 2 to each oval. Chill for ½ hour. I would not suggest putting them in the freezer.

Melt the chocolate in a double boiler. Watch your temperatures (I never go over 89 degrees). It helps to put your face really close to the pot—you will get chocolate up your nose and increase your popularity. Okay. I lied. You won't be popular with brown stuff on your nose.

Dip each candy-dandy-licious ball into the chocolate; coat evenly and completely. Place on a wax paper–lined cookie sheet until chocolate is set.

My friend Jerri shared a marvelous recipe with me for homemade Mounds bars. We now make them into balls and dip them at Christmas every year. It's a bold and delightful tradition.

MAGIC STRAWBERRY ALMOND MILK SHAKE FUDGE MIX

2 lbs. powdered sugar (about 7 cups)

1 cup Honevyille powdered butter

3 cups Honeyville strawberry milk powder

1 tsp. salt

1 tsp. almond flavoring

Directions: Combine all ingredients until well blended. Place in a gallon-sized freezer bag. I store the bags in the fridge or freezer. Great gift for the holidays! When the holiday gets closer, I simply slip the mix into a fabric bag with the mixing directions printed on a cute tag. Give it away not just for the winter holidays but for Mother's Day, Father's Day, and so on.

To make: Put mix in a microwave-safe bowl with ¾ cup water and heat about 2 minutes. Stir well. Heat one more minute. In the meantime line an 8 × 8 cake pan with foil and then spray the foil with nonstick coating. Pour the melted mix into the foil-lined pan and top with nuts or dried fruit if desired. Leave pan out to cool 3–4 hours or overnight. Remove fudge from the pan and remove from the foil. Cut into 1-inch squares.

Yields 4 dozen love bombs, about 4 pounds of strawberry fudge.

To make into 4 mixes: Simply divide the mix into 4. This will yield about 2½ cups per mix. Cooking directions: use 2 tablespoons water and a small mini-loaf pan instead of the 8 × 8 pan.

When I first tasted the Honevyille strawberry milk powder, I knew that it needed to be in fudge! This milk shake fudge will really make you happy. Dip it in chocolate and it is beautiful.

PEANUT BUTTER FUDGE

PEANUT BUTTER FUDGE MIX

8 cups Honeyville powdered sugar

1 cup Honeyville powdered butter

3 cups Honeyville peanut butter powder

1 tsp. salt

2 tsp. vanilla powder

Directions: Combine all ingredients until well blended. Place in a gallon-sized freezer bag. I store the bags in the fridge or freezer. Great gift for the holidays! When the holiday gets closer, I simply slip the mix into a fabric bag with the mixing directions printed on a cute tag. Give it away not just for the winter holidays, but for Mother's Day, Father's Day, Tuesday.

To make: Put mix in a microwave-safe bowl with ¾ cup water and heat about 2 minutes. Stir well. Heat one more minute. In the meantime line an 8 × 8 cake pan with foil and then spray the foil with nonstick coating. Pour the melted mix into the foil-lined pan and top with nuts or dried fruit if desired. Leave pan out to cool 3–4 hours or overnight. Remove fudge from the pan and remove from the foil. Cut into 1-inch squares.

Yields 4 dozen love bombs, about 4 pounds of peanut butter fudge.

To make into 4 mixes: Simply divide the mix into 4. This will yield about 3 cups per mix. Cooking directions: use 2 tablespoons water and a small mini-loaf pan instead of the 8 × 8 pan.

This mix is crazy fun! Who knew that powdered peanut butter could also be made into a delicious goodie like this? Plus the convenience of a mix is outstanding.

MY FAVORITE ENGLISH TOFFEE

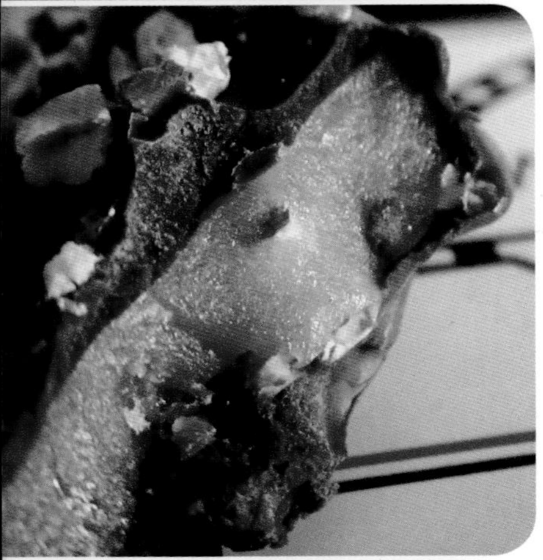

- 2 cups butter (1 lb.)
- 2 cups Honeyville White Satin granulated sugar
- 1 Tbsp. light corn syrup
- 1 cup high-quality milk chocolate chips
- 1 cup toasted pecans (optional)

Directions: Grease a 15 × 10 × 1 baking pan with nonstick coating. In a heavy, 3-quart saucepan, melt the butter. Add the sugar and corn syrup. Stir over medium heat until a candy thermometer reads 295 degrees, hard crack stage. Quickly pour into the prepared pan. Let stand at room temperature about 30 minutes and then top with chocolate chips and smooth them out over the candy when melted. Sprinkle with pecans, if desired. Let stand 2 hours. Break into bite-sized pieces. Store in an airtight container at room temperature.

Yields about 2 pounds toffee. (Yeah, 2 pounds. Mind you, it will put more than 2 pounds on your bum should you eat all the toffee yourself!)

Note: Test your candy thermometer before use by bringing water to a rolling boil. It should read 212 degrees. Water boils at a lower temperature at higher altitudes, so adjust your recipe according to the number on your thermometer.

My husband gets these from me every year for Christmas, and it's as close as he gets to a house made of toffee, which he would take if it wouldn't get bugs. This one is for Ace, my dear honey, who would do just about anything for toffee.

GOURMET MIXES

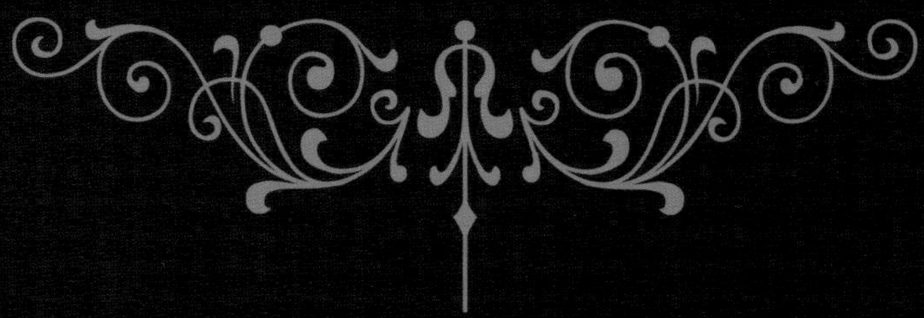

INTRODUCTION TO MIX MAKING

Somewhere along the way I got famous for making shelf-stable mixes that were simple to prepare at home from simple ingredients. In this section I hope to share with you some remarkable secret recipes to help you with not only making convenience mixes for using at home, but also for holiday gift-giving as well.

Why Should You Make Mixes?

- They are budget friendly.
- You can control the ingredients.
- They show creativity.
- They are convenient to give and receive (I don't need to eat them right away).
- They save time.
- They are easily incorporated into long-term food storage.

How Do You Package Mixes?

- Mason jars and up-cycled glass jars
- gift bags, lunch sacks, or goodie bags
- gift basket sets
- up-cycled containers (tins, canisters, boxes, and more)
- fabric bags

CHEF TESS ALL-PURPOSE BAKING MIX

- 9 cups Honeyville all-purpose flour or *Honeyville whole wheat pastry flour
- 2 cups Honeyville shortening powder or Honeyville butter powder
- 1/3 cup baking powder
- 4 tsp. salt
- 1 cup Honeyville powdered milk (optional)

Directions: Combine all ingredients very well. Store in an airtight container.

**Whole wheat flour will require an addition of about 2 Tbsp. of water per 1 cup baking mix called for due to the fiber content and it's amazing ability to soak up the water.*

This recipe is one that I use as a base for many other recipes in this mix-making section, including biscuits, pancakes, muffins, cobblers, and scones. It is remarkably versatile to have on-hand and very easy to make. There are not any extra added chemicals and you control the cost.

BASIC BISCUITS FROM BAKING MIX

2 cups Chef Tess All-Purpose Baking Mix (pg. 171)

½–¾ cup cold water

Directions: Preheat oven to 425 degrees. Combine baking mix and water (all-purpose flour takes less water than whole wheat) until just combined. Roll out on a lightly floured countertop until ¾ inch thick. Cut into 12 small biscuits or 6 large biscuits. Place on an ungreased baking sheet and bake 10–12 minutes.

For added flavor you may use up to 1 Tbsp. seasoning, freeze-dried cheese, or dehydrated green onion mixed into the dry ingredients before adding water. Be creative.

PANCAKES FROM BAKING MIX

2 cups Chef Tess All-Purpose Baking Mix (pg. 171)

1 cup water

Directions: Combine baking mix with water and stir until just combined. Use less water for thick pancakes, more water for thin pancakes. Bake on a hot, lightly oiled griddle. For flavored pancakes, you can use up to ½ cup freeze-dried berries. Let batter sit 5 minutes before making pancakes. For a nice spiced pancake, use ½ teaspoon Chef Tess Wise Woman of the East spice blend or ginger powder.

BASIC UNSWEETENED MUFFINS

¾ cup water

1½ cups Chef Tess All-Purpose Baking Mix (pg. 171)

2 Tbsp. Honeyville egg powder

Directions: Preheat oven to 425 degrees. Add water to the dry ingredients in a medium bowl. Stir until just combined. Scoop into lined muffin cups and bake for 15–20 minutes. (Add ⅓ cup sugar for sweet muffins.)

BASIC COBBLER MIX

1¾ cup Chef Tess All-Purpose Baking Mix (pg. 171)

1 tsp. powdered vanilla

⅓ cup sugar or Honeyville granulated fructose

Directions: Combine the baking mix with vanilla and sugar or fructose.

To make: Combine cobbler dry mixture with ¾ cup water; mix just until combined. Put 4 cups of fruit or fruit pie filling in a 9 × 9 casserole dish. Pour cobbler mixture over filling. Bake at 375 degrees for 35–40 minutes.

BASIC ROLLED SCONE MIX

2 cups Chef Tess All-Purpose Baking Mix (pg. 171)

½ cup sugar

flavor agent of choice

Directions: Combine the baking mix and sugar. To that mixture, add a flavor agent of your choice. I like using one or two of these: 1 Tbsp. cinnamon, ¼ cup currants, ½ cup dried cherries, 1 cup chocolate chips.

To make: Preheat oven to 425 degrees. Add ½ cup water to scone mix. Roll out in circle ½ inch thick and cut into wedges. Bake 10–12 minutes. Spread with butter while warm and sprinkle with infused sugar (I love vanilla sugar with rose petal and cardamom).

VARIATIONS ON HONEYVILLE PANCAKE MIX

Honeyville pancake mix makes an excellent substitute for homemade mix and can easily be turned into gourmet pancake mixes to give during the holidays or any day of the week! I put 2 cups of Honeyville pancake mix in goody baggies and include any of the following variations. Always include preparation directions to the bag of mix.

To make pancakes: Preheat electric griddle to 375 degrees. Combine pancake mix with 1½ cups water (add more or less water depending on how thick you like your pancakes). Oil griddle and bake pancakes. Serve with syrup, cream, and nuts if desired.

SPICED PEACH PECAN PANCAKES

1 scoop Honeyville peaches and cream smoothie mix

½ cup chopped pecans

1 tsp. Chef Tess Wise Woman of The East spice blend

PEANUT BUTTER CHOCOLATE CHIP PANCAKES

3 Tbsp. dehydrated peanut butter

½ cup mini chocolate chips

GINGER MIXED BERRY ALMOND PANCAKES

- 1 scoop Honeyville wild berry smoothie mix
- ½ cup chopped almonds
- ½ tsp. ginger
- ½ tsp. Chef Tess Wise Woman of the East spice blend

APPLE SPICE 6-GRAIN PANCAKES

- ½ cup Honeyville 6 grain rolled cereal
- ¼ cup Honeyville freeze-dried apple, crushed or pulsed in a spice mill to be a powder
- ½ tsp. Chef Tess Wise Woman of the East spice blend

SPICED SWEET POTATO PANCAKES

- ½ cup Honeyville freeze-dried sweet potato, pulsed in a spice mill until a powder
- 1 tsp. Chef Tess Wise Woman of the East spice blend
- 1 tsp. vanilla or maple powder

VARIATIONS ON BUTTERMILK COOKIE MIX

Cookie mixes are a great money-saving and time-saving thing to have on hand. Mixing your own, you can control all the ingredients. Be creative! Add nuts, dried fruit, spices, and flavorings. I'm giving you my basic buttermilk cookie mix to play with, along with some of my favorite flavor variations. I hope this will empower you to create more varieties of your own as well. The cookie-sky is the limit!

CHEF TESS BUTTERMILK COOKIE MIX

- 9 cups all-purpose flour or 9-grain flour
- 1¼ cups Honeyville whole egg powder
- 1¼ cups Honeyville buttermilk powder or instant milk powder
- 1½ cups Honeyville vanilla pudding mix
- 3 Tbsp. baking powder
- 1 Tbsp. salt
- 4 cups Honeyville butter powder
- 2 Tbsp. pure vanilla or LorAnn Princess emulsion (optional)
- 3 cups sugar or Honeyville dehydrated honey

Directions: Combine all ingredients well. This mix will make 20 cups of cookie mix. I use 2 cups of mix per gourmet cookie mix.

This recipe will make 10 pint-size storage bags of plain sugar cookie mix.

MACADAMIA NUT COCONUT LIME COOKIE MIX

- 2 tsp. lime zest, finely grated, dehydrated 24 hours in a dry room
- 2 cups Chef Tess Buttermilk Cookie Mix (pg. 177)
- ½ cup macadamia nuts
- 1 cup white chocolate chips
- ½ cup coconut flakes

Directions: Combine the zest with the cookie mix. Put in a quart-size storage bag or Mason jar. Top with macadamia nuts, chocolate chips, and coconut flakes. Seal tightly.

To bake: Preheat oven to 375 degrees. Combine mix with ⅓ cup water. Form dough into one-inch balls. Place on a cookie sheet one inch apart. Bake 8–10 minutes.

PEANUT BUTTER TOFFEE CRUNCH COOKIE MIX

- 2 cups Chef Tess Buttermilk Cookie Mix (pg. 177)
- ¼ cup Honeyville powdered peanut butter
- ¼ cup Heath Bar bits

Directions: Combine ingredients well. Put in quart-sized storage bag or Mason jar.

To bake: Preheat oven to 375 degrees. In a medium-sized bowl, combine cookie mix with ⅓ cup water. Mix just until combined. Drop by tablespoons on ungreased cookie sheets, 1 inch apart. Bake 8–10 minutes until golden brown.

ORANGE DARK CHOCOLATE 4-GRAIN COOKIE MIX

2 cups Chef Tess Buttermilk Cookie Mix (pg. 177)

1 cup Honeyville 4 grain rolled cereal (or quick oats)

1 cup dark chocolate chips

2 tsp. dry orange zest or orange-flavored powder

Directions: Put 2 cups cookie mix in a quart-sized storage bag or Mason jar. Add a layer of 4-grain cereal, a layer of chocolate chips, and the orange zest. Seal tight.

To bake: Preheat oven to 375 degrees. Combine cookie mix with ½ cup water. Drop dough by rounded tablespoon on ungreased cookie sheet and bake 10–12 minutes.

HOMEMADE BROWNIE MIX

1¼ cup Honeyville all-purpose flour

1 cup Honeyville dehydrated butter

⅔ cup Honeyville whole egg powder

1 tsp. salt

⅔ cup cocoa powder

1 cup white sugar

½ cup chocolate chips

2 Tbsp. Honeyville vanilla pudding mix

Directions: Combine all ingredients and blend well.

To bake: Preheat oven to 350 degrees. Grease a 9 × 13 pan. Empty brownie mix into a large mixing bowl and stir to blend. Mix in ¾ cup water, just until combined. Mix thoroughly. Spread batter evenly into prepared baking pan. Bake for 25 minutes. Cool completely in pan before cutting.

Another one of my favorite mixes is homemade fudge brownie mix. This one is rich and thick. It's more like fudge and less like cake. It's one of my all time favorite desserts.

HOMEMADE BROWNIE

VARIATIONS ON HONEYVILLE BROWNIE MIX

Honeyville makes a very good fudge brownie mix, and I have found buying it in bulk to be a great way to save money as well as create some new twists on the plain fudge brownie. As amazing as the regular fudge brownie mix is, it's nice to have some gourmet additions. The brownie mix comes in a 7-pound bag. From it, you will get 3 gourmet mixes if you measure 4½ cups of mix per your custom blend. I've listed some of my favorite flavor variations here. I think you'll like them.

PECAN TURTLE BROWNIE MIX

Dry mix:

- 4½ cups Honeyville fudge brownie mix
- 1 cup chopped pecans

To prepare mix, you will need:

- 2 eggs
- ¼ cup water
- ½ cup vegetable oil
- 1 cup Kraft caramel bits

Directions: Preheat oven to 325 degrees. In a bowl, combine dry mix ingredients with eggs, water, and vegetable oil. Mix until well combined. Spread into a greased 9 × 13 baking sheet. Bake 30–35 minutes. Remove from oven and top with caramel bits while still warm.

PEANUT BUTTER FUDGE BROWNIE MIX

Dry mix:

- 4½ cups Honeyville fudge brownie mix
- ½ cup Honeyville dehydrated peanut butter
- 1 cup salted peanuts

To prepare mix you will need:

- 2 eggs
- ¼ cup water
- ½ cup vegetable oil

Directions: Preheat oven to 325 degrees. In a bowl, combine dry mix ingredients with eggs, water, and vegetable oil. Mix until well combined. Spread into a greased 9 × 13 baking sheet. Bake 30–35 minutes.

RASPBERRY RED VELVET AND WHITE CHOCOLATE BROWNIES

RASPBERRY RED VELVET AND WHITE CHOCOLATE BROWNIE MIX

Dry mix:

4½ cups Honeyville fudge brownie mix

1 packet raspberry Kool-Aid

½ tsp. dehydrated orange zest

½ cup Honeyville freeze-dried raspberries, crushed

1 cup white chocolate chips or chunks

To prepare mix you will need:

2 eggs

¼ cup water

½ cup vegetable oil

Directions: Preheat oven to 325 degrees. Combine dry mix ingredients. In a bowl, combine mixture with eggs, water, and vegetable oil. Mix until well combined. Spread into a greased 9 × 13 baking sheet. Bake for 30–35 minutes.

HOMEMADE WHOLE GRAIN CAKE MIX

If you are looking for a more natural alternative to the cake mixes at the store, this is my "go-to" recipe. It will replace any boxed cake mix and save you a lot of money in the process.

- 5 cups whole grain cake flour* (I use Honeyville 9 grain cereal made into a flour)
- 2½ cups sugar (or Xylitol natural sweetener)
- 2 Tbsp. baking powder
- 1 Tbsp. salt
- 1 cup organic shortening or butter
- 1 Tbsp. double strength vanilla

Directions: Sift flour, sugar, baking powder, and salt through a flour sifter at least once to remove extra lumps. Combine shortening (or butter) with dry ingredients and vanilla in a KitchenAid-type mixer with paddle attachment. Mix until well combined. If you don't have a mixer, it also works to cut the shortening into the flour as you would for pie crust and then run the mix through a handheld flour sifter to make the mixture more smooth. The metal flour sifters are available to purchase at most grocery stores and baking sections of Walmart or Target. If you use butter, keep your mix in the fridge!

Yields 9 cups cake mix.

(4½-cup mix equal to one store-purchased boxed cake mix)

**Soft white wheat flour or spelt flour will work. Wheat bread flour is not a good alternative for cake mix. The protein content is too high to produce a tender cake.*

To prepare mix, you will need:

- 1/3 cup oil
- 1 1/3 cup water
- 3 eggs or 6 Tbsp. Honeyville powdered egg hydrated with ¾ cup water

To bake: Preheat oven to 350 degrees. Combine 4½ cups of cake mix with oil, water, and eggs or powdered egg. Mix 200 strokes by hand or 3 minutes medium speed.

Pan size and bake time at 350 degrees:

- (2) 8-inch: 33–35 minutes
- (2) 9-inch: 28–31 minutes
- 13-inch by 9-inch: 32–35 minutes
- Bundt: 38–43 minutes
- 24 cupcakes: 18–21 minutes

High altitude: Stir ¼ cup all-purpose flour into mix. Mix as directed.

CHEF TESS GOURMET CHOCOLATE CAKE MIX

Dry mix:

- 2 cups Honeyville powdered butter
- 6 cups Honeyville cake flour
- 3 cups baking cocoa
- 1 cup Honeyville instant nonfat milk powder
- 5 cups granulated sugar
- 4 tsp. salt
- 1/3 cup baking powder
- 1 Tbsp. vanilla powdered flavoring
- 1 tsp. ground cardamom
- 1 tsp. cayenne pepper

Directions: In a 3-gallon or larger bowl, combine all ingredients. Divide into quart-size bags. 20 oz. of mix equals one cake mix. This is almost exactly 4 cups of measured mix.

To prepare mix, you will need:

- 3 eggs or 6 Tbsp. Honeyville powdered egg hydrated with 3/4 cup water
- 1/3 cup oil
- 1 cup water

To bake: Preheat oven to 350 degrees. Combine 4 cups of cake mix with eggs or powdered egg, oil, and water. Mix 200 strokes by hand or 3 minutes medium speed.

Pan size and bake time at 350 degrees:

- (2) 8-inch: 33–35 minutes
- (2) 9-inch: 28–31 minutes
- 13-inch by 9-inch: 32–35 minutes
- Bundt: 38–43 minutes
- 24 cupcakes: 18–21 minutes

High altitude: Stir ¼ cup all-purpose flour into mix. Mix as directed.

Yields 18 cups mix (4½ mixes total).

DOUBLE CHOCOLATE HAZELNUT COOKIE MIX

Dry mix:

- 4 cups Chef Tess Gourmet Chocolate Cake Mix (pg. 188)
- 2 Tbsp. Honeyville dehydrated egg powder
- 1 cup chocolate chips (high quality)
- ½ cup chopped hazelnuts

To prepare, you will need:

- ½ cup water
- ¼ cup melted butter

Directions: To bake, preheat oven to 350 degrees. Combine dry mix ingredients. Combine mixture with water and melted butter in a bowl. Drop by heaping tablespoons onto greased cookie sheets. Bake until set but still soft in the center, 8–10 minutes. Remove cookies from oven and let cookies cool on pan 2–3 minutes. Remove from pan and cool completely.

WHITE CHOCOLATE SUN-DRIED CHERRY ALMOND CHEWY COOKIE MIX

Dry mix:

- 4 cups Chef Tess Gourmet Chocolate Cake Mix (pg. 188)
- 2 Tbsp. Honeyville whole egg powder
- 1 cup white chocolate chips
- ½ cup chopped almonds
- ½ cup seedless sun-dried cherries

To prepare, you will need:

- ½ cup water
- ¼ cup melted butter.

Directions: To bake, place rack in center of oven. Preheat to 350 degrees. Combine dry mix ingredients. Combine mixture with water and melted butter. Drop dough by rounded tablespoons onto greased cookie sheet and bake 8–10 minutes. Remove from oven. Allow to cool 2–3 minutes on pan. Transfer to a cooling rack and cool completely.

CHOCOLATE-DIPPED MACAROON BARS

Crust mix:

4 cups Chef Tess Chocolate Cake Mix (pg. 188)

2 Tbsp. Honeyville powdered whole eggs

½ tsp. almond extract

1 cup melted butter

¼ cup water

½ cup cool water

1 cup semisweet chocolate chips

Macaroon Topping mix:

1½ cup Honeyville macaroon coconut

¼ cup Honeyville powdered whole eggs

Directions: Preheat oven to 350 degrees. Combine crust mix ingredients. Mix melted butter and ¼ cup water with crust mix. Spread into the bottom of a 9 × 13 baking pan. The batter will be thick. Combine topping ingredients with ½ cup cool water and mix until very blended. Spread over the chocolate crust mixture. Sprinkle with chocolate chips. Bake until the coconut mixture sets, 25–30 minutes. Remove from oven and cool 1 hour before cutting into bars.

Yields 24 bars.

VARIATIONS ON HONEYVILLE YELLOW WHITE CAKE MIX

Honeyville yellow white cake mix not only makes great cake, but it can be used for dessert mixes as well. Here are a few of my favorite mix recipes!

WISE WOMAN'S SNICKERDOODLE BLONDIE MIX

Dry mix:

- 4 cup Honeyville yellow white cake mix
- ¼ cup Honeyville whole egg powder.

Spiced sugar mix:

- 1 Tbsp. Chef Tess Wise Woman of the East blend
- ¼ cup sugar

To prepare, you will need:

- ½ cup melted real butter
- ½ cup water

Directions: Preheat oven to 350 degrees. Grease a 9 × 13 baking pan. Combine dry mix ingredients together. Separately, combine spiced sugar mix ingredients. Combine dry mix with melted butter and water until just combined. Spread into baking pan. Sprinkle with spiced sugar mix. Bake 25–30 minutes.

I grew up eating snickerdoodle cookies and always loved the cinnamon-sugar coating with the tender, almost fudgy texture of the lightly tart sugar cookies. Imagine my joy in discovering how magnificent these were as a fast and easy bar mix instead of a labor-intensive cookie! Try them with my Wise Woman of the East spice blend. You might just cry tears of joy.

JAM CRUMBLE BAR MIX

Dry mix:

- 4 cups Honeyville yellow white cake mix
- 1 cup sugar
- 1 cup Honeyville quick oats
- ½ cup Honeyville flax seeds
- ¼ cup Honeyville whole egg powder
- 1 tsp. Chef Tess Wise Woman of the East spice blend

To prepare, you will need:

- ¼ cup water
- ½ cup melted butter
- 2 cups jam (any flavor)

Directions: Preheat oven to 350 degrees. Combine dry mix ingredients. Place mix in a large bowl and combine with water and melted butter until blended. The mixture will be thick. Reserve 1½ cups of the mixture. Using fingertips, press the remaining mixture into the bottom of a 9 × 13 baking pan so it reaches all sides. Spread the jam over the mixture in a layer with a spatula. Pinch off pieces of the reserved crust mixture and scatter over the jam. Bake until light brown and bubbling, 35–40 minutes. Allow to cool 30 minutes before cutting.

Yields 24 bars.

JAM CRUMBLE BAR

BUTTERSCOTCH PISTACHIO SCOTCHIES MIX

Bar mix:

- 4 cups Honeyville yellow white cake mix
- ¼ cup Honeyville granulated honey
- ¼ cup Honeyville powdered whole eggs
- 1 tsp. butterscotch-flavored oil or powder

To prepare, you will need:

- ½ cup water
- ½ cup melted butter
- 1 cup salted pistachios
- 1 cup butterscotch chips

Directions: Preheat oven to 350 degrees. Combine bar mix ingredients together. Combine with water and melted butter in a bowl until smooth, about 2 minutes by hand. Transfer batter to 9 × 13 baking pan, spreading evenly. Sprinkle the bars with pistachios and butterscotch chips. Bake until golden brown, 27–29 minutes. Allow to cool 30 minutes before cutting.

Yields 24 bars.

DANDY CANDY BAR MIX

Bar mix:

- 4 cups Honeyville yellow white cake mix
- ½ cup Honeyville granulated honey
- ¼ cup Honeyville powdered whole eggs
- ¼ cup Honeyville powdered butter
- 2 cups chopped candy bar pieces (Butterfinger, Mounds, Almond Joy, Snickers, Zero, or Reese's)

To prepare, you will need:

- ½ cup melted butter
- ½ cup water

Directions: Preheat oven to 350 degrees. Combine bar mix ingredients together. Combine with melted butter and water until just combined. Spread mixture into a well-greased 9 × 13 pan. Sprinkle with candy bar pieces. Bake until golden brown, 40–45 minutes. Remove from oven and allow to cool about 1 hour before cutting.

Yields 24 bars.

MULLED APPLE CIDER BUNDT CAKE WITH LEMON GLAZE

MULLED APPLE CIDER BUNDT CAKE MIX WITH LEMON GLAZE

Dry mix:

4 cups Honeyville yellow white cake mix

½ cup Honeyville vanilla pudding mix

½ cup Honeyville powdered whole eggs

1½ tsp. Chef Tess Wise Woman of the East spice blend

2 cups high-quality apple cider

½ cup olive oil

Glaze mix:

1 cup Honeyville powdered sugar

1 Tbsp. Honeyville lemonade powder

2 Tbsp. hot water

Directions: Preheat oven to 350 degrees. Lightly mist Bundt pan with nonstick spray and dust with flour. Shake out excess flour and set pan aside. Combine dry cake mix ingredients. Place the cake mix in a mixer and combine with apple cider and olive oil, mixing on low speed for 30 seconds and then increasing to medium speed for 2 minutes, scraping down sides again. The batter should be thick and well combined. Pour into your prepared pan. Bake 42–48 minutes. Remove pan from oven and place on wire rack to cool 10 minutes. While cake bakes, prepare the glaze by combining the sugar and lemonade powder with hot water and stirring until smooth. Invert the cake onto a platter while it is still warm and pour the glaze over the cake. Garnish with spices and fruit if desired. Slice and serve.

During autumn and winter months, I love to give a spiced apple cider cake to friends and family. It is a glorious and richly spiced, moist cake that whispers of all things merry and bright. When it's baking, the smell fills the air with happiness.

In the spring and summer, there's something classic about a lemon pound cake coupled with fresh berries or a fruit compote. When I developed this recipe, I wanted a cake that would stay moist for several days and still be outstanding to serve to any honored guest in my home or to take to a group gathering and still get gasps of joy coming from my friends. So, here's the recipe that won my heart. It's rich, thick, exceptionally moist, and full of great flavor.

LEMON SOUR CREAM POUND CAKE MIX WITH MIXED BERRY CREAM GLAZE

Dry mix:

- 4½ cups Honeyville yellow white cake mix
- ¾ cup Honeyville lemonade powder (any flavor)
- 1 cup Honeyville powdered sour cream
- ½ cup Honeyville powdered whole eggs

To prepare cake you will need:

- 2 cups water

Glaze:

- ½ cup Honeyville margarine powder
- 1 scoop Honeyville wild berry smoothie mix
- ¼ cup Honeyville lemonade powder (any flavor)
- ½ cup powdered sugar
- ¼ cup hot water
- 1 tsp. vanilla

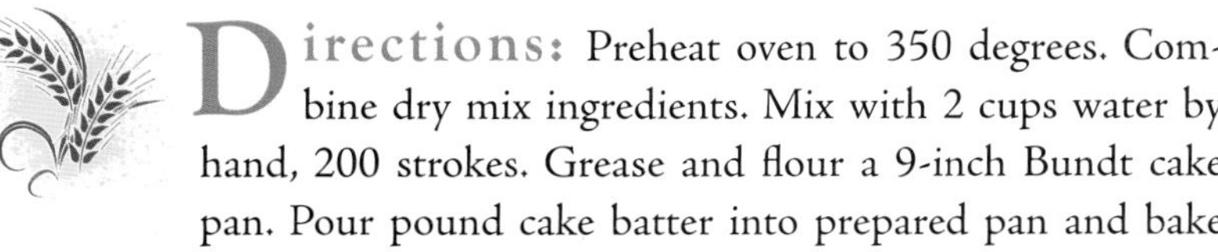

Directions: Preheat oven to 350 degrees. Combine dry mix ingredients. Mix with 2 cups water by hand, 200 strokes. Grease and flour a 9-inch Bundt cake pan. Pour pound cake batter into prepared pan and bake 55–65 minutes until a toothpick comes out clean. Cool in pan 20 minutes before inverting.

For the glaze: Combine dry ingredients and put through a sifter to ensure there are no lumps. Put in a medium-sized bowl. Add the hot water and vanilla. Stir until smooth. Drizzle over cake.

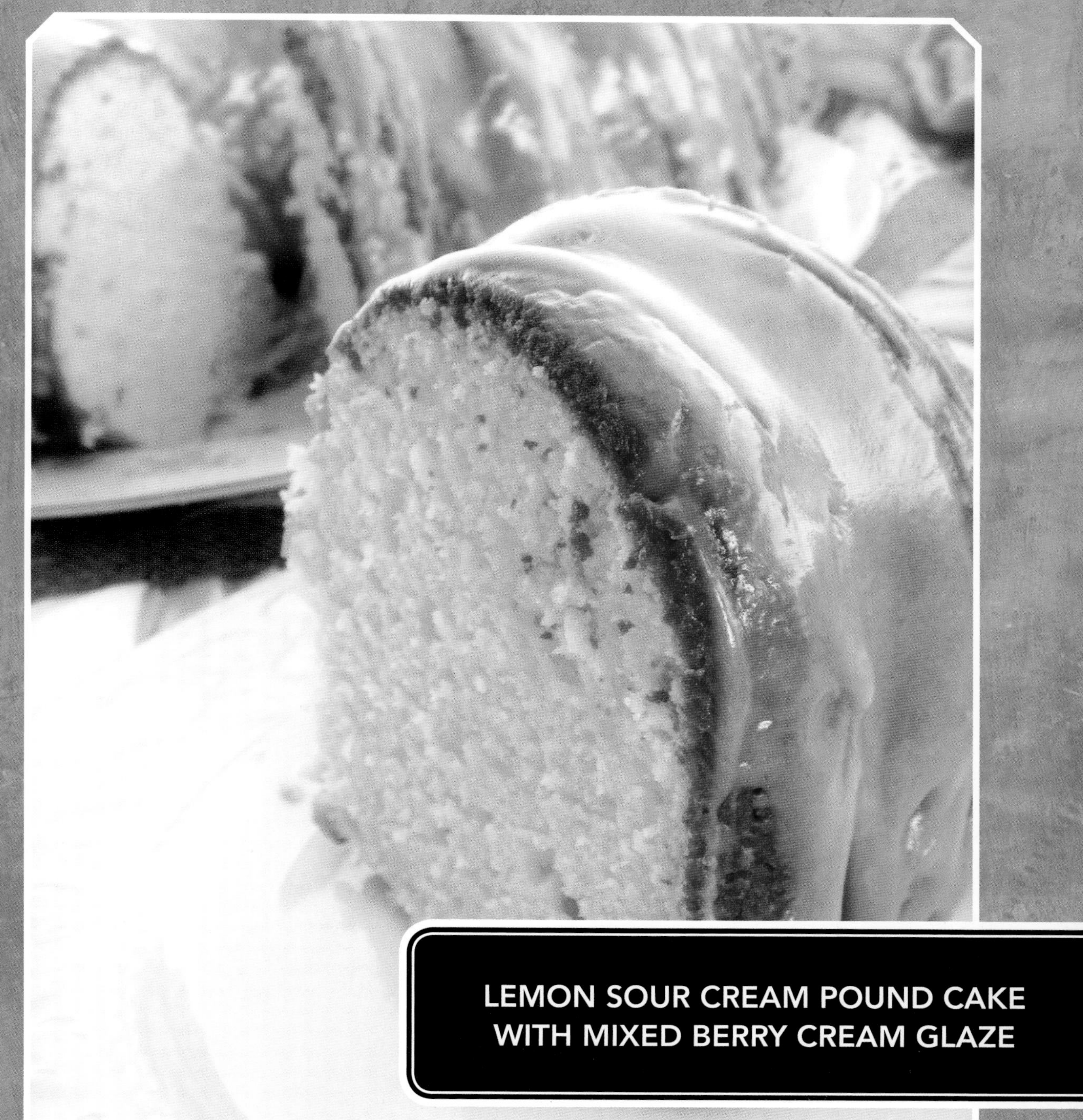

LEMON SOUR CREAM POUND CAKE WITH MIXED BERRY CREAM GLAZE

GOURMET PARADISE OATMEAL MAC-NUT COOKIE MIX

Dry mix:

- 4 cups Honeyville yellow white cake mix
- ¼ cup Honeyville powdered whole eggs
- 1 cup Honeyville all-purpose flour
- ¾ cup Honeyville quick oats
- ¼ cup crushed cornflakes
- ¼ cup Honeyville coconut flakes
- 1 cup whole macadamia nuts
- 1 cup white chocolate chips

To prepare cookies you will need:

- ¾ cup melted butter
- ½ cup water

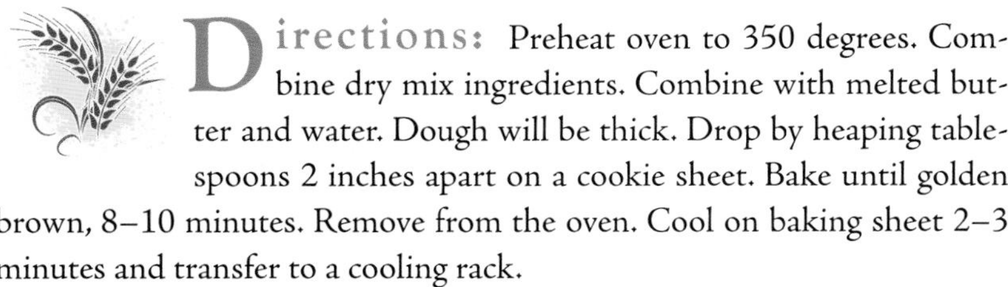

Directions: Preheat oven to 350 degrees. Combine dry mix ingredients. Combine with melted butter and water. Dough will be thick. Drop by heaping tablespoons 2 inches apart on a cookie sheet. Bake until golden brown, 8–10 minutes. Remove from the oven. Cool on baking sheet 2–3 minutes and transfer to a cooling rack.

HOLIDAY SOUP MIXES

WARM AND BRIGHT HOLIDAY GREETINGS

CREAMY TOMATO SOUP MIX

- ½ cup Honeyville all-purpose flour or ¼ cup cornstarch
- 1½ cup Honeyville nonfat dry milk powder
- ½ cup Honeyville tomato powder
- 1 bay leaf
- 1 Tbsp. Honeyville dehydrated onions
- ¼ tsp. celery seed
- 2 tsp. granulated garlic
- 2 tsp. salt
- 1 tsp. baking soda
- 2 tsp. pepper
- 2 tsp. thyme
- 2 Tbsp. MSG-free bouillon (optional) (omit salt if you use bouillon)

Directions: In a quart jar layer all ingredients. Top with an oxygen absorber packet and seal lid tightly.

To make: Remove oxygen absorber packet and discard. Combine soup mix with 6 cups water (for a richer cream soup, use milk) and whisk over medium heat until combined. Simmer 15–20 minutes. Add any flavor variations you like: 2 cups chopped broccoli, cauliflower, potatoes, corn, carrots, chicken, clams, or crumbled bacon. If you want a cheese soup, be sure cheese gets added only at the end, after soup is off the heat, or it will be grainy.

give the soup mix
r wrapped in a shiny
aper and tied with
gold bow. In a gift
asket, I'll include a
ooden spoon with a
ed handle tied with
ngham and some
arlic-cheese biscuit
nix. I keep this mix in
rs sealed and labeled
or a quick dinner
nytime of the year.
hey keep fresh up to a
ear (for best flavor), so
lease be sure to label
nd date clearly. The
aking soda will keep
he milk from curdling
n your pan when
nixed with the tomato.
's magic!

COUNTRY-STYLE HOLIDAY GREETINGS

COUNTRY-STYLE BEEF STEW MIX

- 1 cup Honeyville quick cook red beans
- 1 cup Honeyville freeze-dried vegetable mix
- ¾ cup Honeyville freeze-dried beef dices
- 1 cup Honeyville dehydrated diced potatoes
- ¼ cup Honeyville dehydrated onions
- ½ cup Honeyville tomato powder
- 1 tsp. thyme
- 1 tsp. garlic
- ¼ cup flour or 2 Tbsp. cornstarch
- 1 Tbsp. beef bouillon (optional)

Directions: Layer first five ingredients in a jar. Shake remaining ingredients into the cracks of the first ingredients. It will fit if you shake it really well. Place an oxygen packet on top of ingredients inside the jar and close tightly using a canning lid and ring.

To make: Remove oxygen packet and discard. In a gallon pot, combine stew mix with 6 cups water and bring to a boil. Reduce heat and simmer 20–30 minutes.

Yields 12 servings.

I give this in a package wrapped in gingham with a few rustic wood ornaments and a wooden spoon. In a gift basket I'll also add some homemade biscuit mix.

WARMEST HOLIDAY GREETINGS

TACO SOUP MIX

- 2 cups Honeyville quick cook red beans
- 1 cup Honeyville taco-flavored TVP
- ½ cup Honeyville dehydrated onions
- ⅓ cup Honeyville freeze-dried bell peppers
- ¾ cup Honeyville freeze-dried corn
- ½ cup Honeyville tomato powder
- 1 Tbsp. taco seasoning

Directions: Add all ingredients to a quart-sized Mason jar one at a time. When you get to the tomato powder and taco seasoning, just shake the jar so it works its way into the cracks. Add an oxygen packet. Seal jar by tightly screwing on the lid. This mix is good on the shelf in a cool place up to 5–7 years.

To make: Remove oxygen packet and discard. Place contents of jar in a gallon pot on the stove. Add 2 quarts water and simmer 20–30 minutes until veggies are tender. Serve with tortilla chips, sour cream, and salsa if desired.

I give this one wrapped in funky red pepper fabric and a raffia bow with a bag of corn chips in a basket. Often, I embellish this one with poinsettia and Mexican yarn puff balls or tissue paper flowers.

CHEESY HOLIDAY GREETINGS

CREAMY POTATO CHEESE AND HAM WITH ROSEMARY SOUP MIX

- 3 cups Honeyville potato cheese soup mix
- 1 cup Honeyville freeze-dried ham (do not use the ham-flavored TVP for this)
- 1 bay leaf
- 1 tsp. dehydrated rosemary
- ½ tsp. cracked black pepper

Directions: Layer ingredients in a quart jar with an oxygen absorber packet at the top of the jar and seal tightly.

To make: Remove oxygen absorber and discard. Combine soup mix with 10 cups cool water. Bring to a boil. Reduce heat and simmer 15–20 minutes, stirring occasionally. Yields 12 cups soup.

I give this one with a bright orange or yellow gingham bow, a small jar of freeze-dried cheddar cheese, and a bag of cheese biscuit mix in a basket.

GLUTEN-FREE

TIPS AND TECHNIQUES ON BAKING GLUTEN-FREE

Are you new to gluten-free baking? Here are some of my favorite tricks for baking outstanding whole grain, gluten-free breads, cookies, and more.

- Use a combination of flours. Usually, one kind of flour will not do the trick for avoiding dense, heavy results. Generally, I plan on using no more than 30 percent of each kind of flour. Usually this means no more than 1½ cups of one kind of flour for every 5 cups of blended flour. The exception: chickpea and millet. They have a strong flavor and will overpower the flavor of baked goods. For these you can use a lot less, about ¾ cup for every 4 to 5 cups of flour blend.
- Use a good formula for healthy all-purpose flour. I use 1½ cups nutrient-dense flour (amaranth, buckwheat, quinoa, sorghum), 1 cup neutral flour (white/brown rice flour, corn flour), 1 cup starch (tapioca, corn, potato), and ½ cup alternate starch.
- Store high-protein flours in airtight containers. Use one with a wide mouth so you can measure over the container. I love a 2-gallon food storage bucket for this. It's just the right size.
- Refrigerate all gluten-free flours. This will keep the oils from going rancid too quickly. Allow refrigerated flours to return to room temperature before you use them, unless the recipe states otherwise.
- Use a wire whisk. It's a great tool to get rid of flour clumps before you measure.

HIGH-PROTEIN FLOUR BLEND

3 cups Honeyville buckwheat flour

2 cups Honeyville brown rice flour

2 cups Honeyville tapioca starch/flour

1 cup Honeyville cornstarch or potato starch

2 Tbsp. xanthan gum

1 Tbsp. sea salt

Directions: Blend ingredients well. Place in tightly sealed container and refrigerate. Each ¼ cup contains 121 calories, 1g total fat, 0g saturated fat, 0g trans fat, 0mg cholesterol, 234mg sodium, 27g carbohydrate, 2g fiber, 2g protein. Makes 7½ cups. Note that most power flours are interchangeable in equal amounts (not flax seed meal, chickpea, or millet flour). Neutral flours are interchangeable in equal amounts. Flours are not interchangeable with starches, as they have different baking properties.

CHEF TESS GLUTEN-FREE, FRESH-MILLED, SUPER-GRAIN FLOUR

- 20 oz. sorghum
- 12 oz. buckwheat
- 12 oz. brown rice
- 12 oz. amaranth
- 12 oz. quinoa (pre-rinsed variety is best and will not impart a bitter flavor to flour)

Directions: Measure the grains by weight. Mix the grain together. Mill the flour on the finest milling setting. If you are not generally gluten free and are milling flour for someone who is, you may need to find out how sensitive they are to gluten. Generally try to have one mill that is 100 percent gluten free. This will keep the flour from being contaminated. For those highly sensitive to gluten, this is very important.

CHEF TESS SUPER-GRAIN, ALL-PURPOSE, GLUTEN-FREE FLOUR

5 cups Chef Tess Gluten-Free, Fresh-Milled, Super-Grain Flour (pg. 212)

2 cups tapioca starch/flour

1 cup Honeyville cornstarch

2 Tbsp. xanthan gum

1 Tbsp. sea salt

Directions: Combine all ingredients and store in an airtight container. Use my super-grain flour in most any recipe that calls for all-purpose flour.

GLUTEN-FREE BREAD

GLUTEN-FREE BREAD

- 1/3 cup egg whites
- 1 egg
- 1 Tbsp. apple cider vinegar
- ¼ cup olive oil
- ¼ cup honey
- 1½ cups warm skim milk or soy milk
- 1 tsp. salt
- 1 Tbsp. xanthan gum
- 1 cup tapioca flour
- 2 cups Chef Tess Super-Grain, All-Purpose, Gluten-Free Flour (pg. 213)
- 1½ cups Honeyville brown rice flour*
- 1 Tbsp. active dry yeast

Directions: Preheat oven to 350 degrees. Combine egg whites, egg, apple cider vinegar, olive oil, honey, and skim milk in a bowl. In a gallon-sized mixer bowl, combine salt, xanthan gum, tapioca flour, Super-Grain flour, and brown rice flour. Add the yeast to the wet ingredients. Combine wet and dry ingredients and knead by hand 3–4 minutes. Form into a rough ball. Allow to sit 5–10 minutes. Sprinkle countertop with ¼ cup extra brown rice flour. Put dough on counter and gently form into a loaf. Place loaf in a lightly greased 8 × 4 bread pan. Leave uncovered to rise on the counter 45 minutes. Bake bread in oven preheated to 350 degrees 60–65 minutes until internal temperature of 170 degrees. When bread is finished, let cool 10–15 minutes before removing from pan. Slice with a sharp bread knife after bread has cooled. Wrap or keep in an airtight container after bread cools to retain moisture.

**Honeyville brown rice flour is packaged in a factory that also processes wheat. It is not certified gluten-free for that reason.*

I searched high and low for good gluten-free bread and never found one that I really loved. So I developed this recipe. It's crusty and delicious with deep flavor and excellent chew! It's just like the bread you left behind to be gluten-free. Remember to wrap it tightly after you bake it. This will keep it moist.

GLUTEN-FREE BROWN RICE CHOCOLATE CHIP BUTTERSCOTCH COOKIES

2½ cups Honeyville brown rice flour*

1 tsp. xanthan gum

1 tsp. salt

1 tsp. baking powder

½ cup melted butter

1½ cups dark brown sugar

2 eggs

1 tsp. pure Bourbon vanilla

2 cup darks chocolate chips or chunks

Directions: Preheat oven to 375 degrees. In a large bowl, combine the brown rice flour, xanthan gum, salt, and baking powder. In a separate bowl, whisk the melted butter, dark brown sugar, eggs, and vanilla. Mix the brown rice flour mixture with the egg and sugar mixture. Stir well. Add the chocolate chips. Scoop cookies onto a lightly oiled cookie sheet with 1 inch between cookies. Lightly flatten cookies with your hand. Bake 9–10 minutes. Remove from oven and allow to cool on cookie sheet 5 minutes before transferring to a cooling rack. Keep in an airtight container.

Yields 2 dozen cookies.

**Honeyville brown rice flour is packaged in a factory that also processes wheat. It is not certified gluten-free for that reason.*

Honeyville brown rice flour makes outstanding cookies that melt in your mouth. These are my favorite chocolate chip confections. They are evil and delicious.

GLUTEN-FREE BROWN RICE ORANGE GINGERBREAD COOKIES

- 3 cups Honeyville brown rice flour*
- 1 tsp. xanthan gum
- 1 tsp. salt
- 1 tsp. baking powder
- 2 tsp. Chef Tess Wise Woman of the East spice blend
- ½ tsp. ground ginger
- 2 tsp. fresh orange zest
- ½ cup olive oil
- 1½ cups dark brown sugar or Honeyville granulated erythritol (natural sweetener)
- 2 Tbsp. molasses
- 2 eggs
- 1 tsp. pure Bourbon vanilla
- sugar (for coating)

Directions: Preheat oven to 375 degrees. In a large bowl, combine the brown rice flour, xanthan gum, salt, baking powder, spice blend, ginger, and orange zest. In a separate bowl, whisk the olive oil, dark brown sugar, molasses, eggs, and vanilla. Mix the brown rice flour mixture with the egg and sugar mixture. Stir well. Mixture will be thick. Scoop cookies (2 Tbsp. each) and round with hands into balls. Roll the balls of dough in sugar. Transfer to a lightly oiled cookie sheet with 1 inch between cookies. Lightly flatten cookies to ½ inch thick with your hand. Bake 9–10 minutes. Remove from oven and allow to cool on cookie sheet 5 minutes before transferring to a cooling rack. Keep in an airtight container.

Yields 2 dozen cookies.

**Honeyville brown rice flour is packaged in a factory that also processes wheat. It is not certified gluten-free for that reason.*

It isn't really the holiday season until I've had a good gingerbread cookie. This is a recipe that I converted, with an added hint of orange, from an old pioneer gingerbread.

GLUTEN-FREE ALMOND FLOUR SUGAR-FREE COOKIES

2 cups Honeyville almond flour

1 cup Honeyville granulated erythritol (natural sweetener)

1 egg

½ tsp. vanilla

¼ tsp. baking soda

Directions: Preheat oven to 350 degrees. Mix together all ingredients. Scoop by rounded tablespoons onto a parchment-lined baking sheet. Dough will be thick. Flatten slightly with a lightly moistened hand. Bake 12–15 minutes. Allow cookies to cool 5 minutes on the pan before removing to a cooling rack.

Yields 18 cookies.

Often the cookie that is missed the most when going gluten-free is the basic sugar cookie. This is a great recipe that is not only gluten free, but also sugar free. It's also great for those who have to watch their carbohydrates. I just adore Honeyville almond flour. It's divine.

GLUTEN-FREE ALMOND FLOUR SUGAR-FREE COOKIES

AUNTIE EM'S SOFT DIVINE GLUTEN-FREE PUMPKIN CHOCOLATE CHIP COOKIES

When my sister, Em, shared these cookies she made, I couldn't help from smiling! They are the perfect pumpkin cookie. Never mind that they are gluten-free and low-sugar and are loaded with the health benefits of pumpkin . and, um, chocolate. They are beautiful! I didn't think they were gluten-free. They were so soft and delightful. I've tasted a lot of gluten-free snacks. These blew me away. So, this one is all Em. She converted my pumpkin cookie recipe into this gluten-free wonder. Thank you, Em!

- 1½ cups butter, softened
- 2 cups brown sugar*
- 1 cup white sugar*
- 2 Tbsp. molasses
- 1 (15-oz.) can solid-pack pumpkin
- 2 eggs
- 2 tsp. vanilla
- 6 cups Chef Tess Super-Grain, All-Purpose, Gluten-Free Flour (pg. 213)
- 1 Tbsp. baking powder
- 1 tsp. salt
- 2 tsp. xanthan gum
- 1 Tbsp. Chef Tess Wise Woman of the East spice blend
- 3 cups gluten-free chocolate chips
- 1 cup walnuts or pecans (optional)

Directions: Preheat oven to 375 degrees. In a large mixing bowl, cream the softened butter, sugars, and molasses. Scrape down the bowl. Add the pumpkin, eggs, and vanilla. Mix well, about 2 minutes. Add the flour, baking powder, salt, xanthan gum, and spice blend. Stir well and add chocolate chips and optional nuts. Drop by rounded tablespoon onto ungreased baking sheet, about 1 inch apart. Bake 10–12 minutes. Remove from baking sheet to a cooling rack.

Yields about 8 dozen cookies.

**For a natural sugar-free cookie, I use 3 cups granular erythritol in place of the sugars in this recipe.*

ALL-NATURAL GLUTEN-FREE PANCAKE MIX

- 4 cups Chef Tess Super-Grain, All-Purpose, Gluten-Free Flour (pg. 213)
- ½ cup organic extra virgin coconut oil (chilled for about 20 minutes until solid)
- ⅓ cup Honeyville granular erythritol
- 2 Tbsp. baking powder
- 1 tsp. salt
- 1 Tbsp. xanthan gum

Directions: Combine ingredients well, until oil is smaller than the size of a pea. Yields 4½ cups (2 mixes).

To prepare, you will need:

- dash of cinnamon or nutmeg
- ½ tsp. vanilla
- 2 eggs
- 3 cups water or soy milk

To make: In a medium-sized bowl, combine 2¼ cups pancake mix, a dash of cinnamon or nutmeg, vanilla, eggs, and water or soy milk. Mix until well combined. Cook on a hot griddle.

Are you ready for some whole grain pancakes that taste great and are still gluten-free? Here's my recipe for those. It makes fluffy, tasty pancakes and waffles. Make waffles ahead of time and freeze them in individual sandwich bags for a quick homemade toaster-waffle that will save you a lot of money.

INDEX

N

O

P

R

S

T

W

Y

Stephanie Petersen (a.k.a. Chef Tess Bakeresse) is a classically trained chef. She ives in Phoenix, Arizona, with her husband and wo children. She has worked in bakeshops, res-aurants, and banquets. When she became a moth-r in 1999, she set aside her work in the restaurant nd focused full-time on her children. At the time, t seemed like such a sacrifice. Ironically, it became preparation for a much higher work. This time away from her career gave her real world experi-ence in not only cooking on a tight budget but earning nutrition and gardening skills. Stephanie nas been a superintendent at a local organic toma-o farm. She is an avid solar cooker and is passion-ate about alternative cooking methods. When her church bishop asked her to teach some of the gals some basic cooking skills, she soon found that she

help them save money and eat nutritional meal She started milling her own spice blends late a night to earn extra money in order to be home with her babies.

When her youngest son started school in the fal of 2008, she started her food blog (cheftessbaker-esse.com) with a borrowed cheap camera and nc idea what she was getting into. It only took a few months before her unique talents with decorative bread and bread-painting techniques were noticec and published in *Australian Baking Business* maga-zine. Just a few months later, she was asked by the Fox 10 Arizona Morning Show if she would b a guest on the show. Thinking it would be a one-time visit, Stephanie went to the TV station. T her astonishment and joy, she has been a regularly featured chef since then and loves getting in fron of the camera! It wasn't long after that first Fo 10 visit that she was also asked to be a regularly featured guest chef and "Idea Extraordinaire" or NBC 12's Phoenix "Valley Dish," with ratings tha beat Oprah when she was featured.

Stephanie has been a large group and persona cooking instructor since 2004 and continues to be heavily involved with culinary education arounc the country. One of her favorite places to teach is, of course, the Honeyville Farms retail stores Stephanie's spices have been bottled by Honeyville Farms, and she feels deeply honored to write this Honeyville cookbook. She is, in every way, a rea down-to-earth gal who adores teaching, laugh-ing, loving, and connecting with new people every day. She can often be found repeating her favorite words to her students, "Onward and upward, m